This peaceful symbol pivots above George Washington's home at Mount Vernon, Virginia.

CAL SACKS

A GUIDE TO AMERICA'S GREATEST HISTORIC PLACES

An updated and revised edition by the Editors of American Heritage Magazine

American Heritage, a division of Forbes Inc., New York, N.Y.

Introduction

In 1813 the State of Pennsylvania, temporarily hard up for cash, proposed to sell off the Old State House, the red-brick shrine we now call Independence Hall. A group of angry Philadelphians protested to the legislature that "the Spot which the Bill proposes to cover with private buildings, is hallowed ... by many strong and impressive recollections." It was, after all, the birthplace of "the only free republic the world has seen." Independence Hall endured, of course — though it was a close shave — and is one of the more than 150 great historic sites included in this special guide.

Our history has been a short one, compared with that of other nations, and we have often been heedless of our past. But our history has also been extraordinarily rich and our landscape is still crowded with its fascinating relics.

Drawing up this compendium of sites has been a delightful but difficult task; delightful because of the breadth of the material, and difficult for the very same reason.

Our objective was simply to list those places which we believed to be the most important for any American interested in revisiting his nation's past. We cannot claim that our candidates for inclusion would be yours. There was too much horse trading — my frigate for your mining town — for us to have any illusions about that.

But we have tried hard to present the most varied possible selection of sites from every era and every region of our countryside. And we hope that as you visit some of the places herein, you will come away with "strong and impressive recollections" of your own.

The Editors

ALABAMA

HORSESHOE BEND NATIONAL MILITARY PARK, *eastcentral Alabama, about 12 miles north of Dadeville on State 49.*

Horseshoe Bend, a 100-acre peninsula formed by a large loop in the Tallapoosa River, was the site of Andrew Jackson's decisive victory over the Creek Nation on March 27, 1814, which ended the Creek War. This battle, the culmination of his campaign against the warring Upper Creeks, or "Red Stick" faction, broke Creek power in the southeastern United States and opened for settlement Creek lands comprising most of the southern parts of Alabama and Georgia. Approximately 900 warriors were killed in the fierce fighting. The 2,040-acre military park contains a visitor center that houses exhibits on Creek culture, frontier life, and the Creek War. The 3-mile road, which loops through the battlefield connecting key sites, has trails and markers designed to enhance the visitor's understanding of the battle.

For further information write: Box 103, Daviston, AL 36256

MONTGOMERY, *central Alabama, on U.S. 80, I–65, I–85*

Known as the Cradle of the Confederacy, Montgomery was the first capital established by the seceding states. One of the city's most important landmarks is the **Alabama State**, or **First Confederate, Capitol** (NHL), a magnificent Greek Revival building constructed in 1851 and similar in design to the National Capitol. In January 1861 a fiery Secession Convention met in the capitol's house of representatives chamber and voted Alabama out of the Union. Early the next month the secessionists met in the capitol's senate chamber to adopt the Provisional Constitution of the Confederacy and to elect Jefferson Davis president of the Confederacy. On February 18, 1861, Davis took the oath of office on the capitol's west portico. Opposite the state capitol stands the **First White House of the Confederacy**—the home of Jefferson Davis and his family when Montgomery was the capital of the Confederacy. It contains original Davis furniture and relics of the War Between the States. The **Old North Hull Historic Area** contains 14 historic buildings that are open as museums, including the antebellum **Ordeman-Shaw House** and the **Campbell-Holtzclaw House,** which is used as a tourist center. The **Dexter Avenue Baptist Church (NHL)** was the site of the beginning of the modern civil rights movement when Martin Luther King, Jr., pastor of the church, organized the Montgomery bus boycott there in 1955.

State Capitol open daily 8–4:30. White House of the Confederacy open daily 8–5

TUSKEGEE

TUSKEGEE INSTITUTE NATIONAL HISTORIC SITE, *U.S. 80*

Chartered by the state of Alabama in 1881, this pioneer Negro educational institution has furthered black economic progress through vocational and industrial training. Its founder and first president was Booker T. Washington, a former slave who became a distinguished educator and reformer. In 1896 George Washington Carver became head of the institute's agricultural department. His achievements include the development of 300 products from peanuts and 118 from sweet potatoes. The **Carver Museum** houses exhibits of

The crumbling White House, occupied from about 1060 to 1300, A.D. was connected to the floor of the Canyon de Chelly by a long-destroyed tower.

U.S. DEPARTMENT OF THE INTERIOR

the scientist's experiments and a history of the Institute. **The Oaks**, which was Dr. Washington's home, is partially restored. Tours of the home are conducted from the museum.
Museum open daily 9–5. For further information write: 399 Old Montgomery Rd., Tuskegee Institute, AL 36088

ALASKA

KLONDIKE GOLD RUSH NATIONAL HISTORICAL PARK, *southeastern Alaska into northwestern Canada*

The town of Skagway grew up as a result of gold discoveries in the Upper Yukon Valley and the Klondike region during the icy winter of 1897–98. Prior to the news of the 1896 gold strike on Klondike Creek, which reached the United States in June 1897, only one cabin stood on the site of Skagway. Soon hordes of eager would-be prospectors swarmed ashore at Skagway, strategically located on a direct route into the gold-bearing region via the Chilkoot Trail or the White Pass routes. Within a few months Skagway could boast a population of some 10,000. The gold rush days are preserved in the Skagway district of this national park. Here are dirt streets, boardwalks, and false-front buildings. Exhibits of these years can be seen at the visitor center and at the nearby **Trail of '98 Museum** in the old federal court building. Of the major routes to the Yukon the Chilkoot Trail is still accessible only by foot. Beginning at Dyea, 9 miles from Skagway, this 33-mile hike is the most challenging way to the Yukon, but it is arduous and takes 4 days. The **White Pass and Yukon Route Railroad** still makes daily trips to Bennett from Skagway and is very scenic. In addition there is a spur of the Alaska Highway that allows the visitor to drive over the White Pass and stop at some of the historical points of interest such as Dead Horse Gulch. Farther north, Dawson—"the City of Gold"—has been restored by the Canadian government to its appearance at the time of the Gold Rush. To appreciate the entire "Trail of '98" story, one should follow the complete route from **Pioneer Square** in Seattle *(see)* to Carcross, Whitehorse, and Dawson in Canada.
For further information write: Box 517, Skagway, AK 99840

NOME, *Arctic Alaska, on south shore of Seward Peninsula*

The main supply center for the neighboring mining districts and native villages, Nome was the site of the now-legendary gold rush. The rush began when the first large gold placer strike was made in September 1898, at Anvil Creek, about 4 miles north of present-day Nome. At the time of the strike, Nome (then called Anvil City) had a population of about 1,700. A gold rush camp quickly sprang up in a tent city extending for 15 miles along the Nome beach. By June 1900 the U.S. Census showed 12,488 people in Nome, and in the next 2 years mining activities spread to the entire Seward Peninsula. Average daily recovery was from $20 to $100 per man. Since then others have mined these beaches with varying results, but 1899 was the banner year with $1 million of gold dust mined. Today Nome's population has shrunk to about 2,000 people. With its unpaved streets and wooden sidewalks, the town retains the "frontier" atmosphere of its gold rush days. The actual **Anvil Creek Gold Discovery Site** (NHL) has long been abandoned.

ARIZONA

CANYON DE CHELLY NATIONAL MONUMENT, *headquarters at Chinle off State 63*

Built directly into or nestled at the base of the sheer red sandstone cliffs of Canyon de Chelly and its offshoots—Canyon del Muerto and Black Rock and Monument canyons—are ruins of several hundred Pueblo Indian villages. Erected between A.D. 350 and 1300, these settlements represent four periods of Indian culture. The earliest tribe, the Basket Makers, or early Anasazi, lived in individual circular houses constructed over pits dug in the ground. From approximately 700 to 1300, Pueblos, or later Anasazi, occupied the area in large apartment-style cliff houses of stone masonry that were connected in compact villages. About 1300 a severe drought forced the Pueblos to migrate to other parts of the Southwest. The canyons were subsequently occupied by the Hopi Indians, relatives of the Pueblos, who cultivated the canyon bottoms. About 1700, warlike Navajo Indians swept down from northern New Mexico and made Canyon de Chelly their chief stronghold. In 1805 a detachment of Spanish troops under Lieutenant Antonio Narbona defeated a band of Navajos who had hidden themselves in a rock shelter now known as **Massacre Cave.** And in 1864 Kit Carson, leading a U.S. cavalry unit, defeated the Navajos and removed the survivors to new lands in New Mexico. This reservation experiment failed, and eventually the Navajos were permitted to return. Today the Navajos keep their summer homes—circular structures of poles and logs called hogans—here. The best known of the cliff dwellings is **White House,** the only site within the monument that tourists may visit without guides. Other ruins are the **Mummy Cave, Antelope House,** and **Standing Cow.**

For further information write: Box 588, Chinle, AZ 86503

NAVAJO NATIONAL MONUMENT, *32 miles southwest of Kayenta off U.S. 160*

Three of the largest and most elaborate of the pueblo cliff dwellings are preserved at this site in the high plateau country of the Southwest. In the early part of the 13th century, the Anasazi farmers of the San Juan basin began to combine their hamlets into large villages; these cliff dwellings, built between A.D. 1225 and 1300, along with a variety of artifacts—especially pottery—of the same period, represent the culmination of Anasazi culture. **Betatakin** (Navajo for "ledge house") is the most accessible ruin and the site of monument headquarters. This structure contains 135 rooms—living quarters, courts, storage areas, granaries, and a kiva, or ceremonial room. Constructed between 1240 and 1282, **Keet Seel** (Navajo for "broken pottery") is the largest of the cliff dwellings, with 350 rooms. **Inscription House** consists of 75 rooms. By 1300 drought and erosion had caused the Anasazi to abandon these homes. Navajos settled in the region in the 19th century.

For further information write: Superintendent, Tonalea, AZ 86044

TOMBSTONE HISTORIC DISTRICT NATIONAL HISTORIC LANDMARK, *off U.S. 80*

Known today as the Town Too Tough to Die, Tombstone earned an unparalleled reputation in the 1880s for its lawlessness and violence.

Currier and Ives celebrated the Union triumph at Pea Ridge with this crowded lithograph. General Franz Sigel rides the white horse at the left.
CHICAGO HISTORICAL SOCIETY

In 1877 the prospector Ed Schieffelin, despite warnings that the only mineral wealth to be found would be his tombstone, ventured into the inhospitable reaches of southeastern Arizona, where he struck a rich silver lode that he named Tombstone. Almost overnight a community of tents, hastily constructed shacks, dance halls, and saloons sprang up around Schieffelin's claim. By 1881 the boom town boasted a population of 7,000 that during the decade more than doubled. Although Tombstone inevitably attracted a large percentage of desperados and gamblers, the town was perhaps the most cultivated city of its day in the Southwest: it featured its own opera house, where some of the world's best actors and musicians performed. Built in 1882, **St. Paul's Episcopal Church** was the first Protestant church to be erected in Arizona. Floods occurring in 1886 and 1887 finally forced the mines to shut down, and by 1900 the city was nearly deserted. Today many old landmarks serve to revivify the community's colorful past. They include the **Bird Cage Theatre,** with its 14 private boxes, which seated the town's leading citizens, suspended from the ceiling; the **Crystal Palace Gambling Casino,** now restored to its former splendor; the **OK Corral** (site of the famous Earp-Clanton gunfight in 1881) and nearby stagecoach house and stable; the **Wyatt Earp Museum,** housing that family's mementos; and the **Tombstone Courthouse,** an imposing Victorian structure dating from 1882 that has been converted into a museum. Near Tombstone's northern limits is the desolate **Boothill Graveyard.**

TUCSON AND VICINITY

SAN XAVIER DEL BAC MISSION NATIONAL HISTORIC LANDMARK, *9 miles south via Mission Road*

This mission has been celebrated as the most beautiful as well as the best-preserved example of mission architecture in the Spanish Southwest. In 1692, the Jesuit missionary Father Eusebio Francisco Kino came upon a Pima Indian village in southern Arizona that he named after his patron saint, Francis Xavier. Kino subsequently introduced cattle ranching to the community and in 1700 he established a mission, which was later destroyed in the Pima Indian revolt of 1751. After 1767 Franciscans took over the mission and attended, from 1783 to 1797, to the construction of the profusely ornamented present church of stucco-covered brick. The church fell into neglect after the Mexican government secularized its missions in 1821. San Xavier del Bac became United States property in the Gadsden Purchase of 1853 and was eventually restored. Today the church is a thriving parish on the San Xavier Indian Reservation.

ARKANSAS

FORT SMITH NATIONAL HISTORIC SITE, *on Rogers Avenue between Second and Third streets*

Established in 1817 as one of the first U.S. military posts in the Louisiana Territory, Fort Smith remained the center of law and order for a vast area of untamed western frontier during some 80 years. Here one can see the stone foundations of the first fort (1817–39) built on this site. An unimposing wooden structure, it was situated at Belle Point, a rocky bluff overlooking the confluence of the Poteau and Arkansas rivers. Its purpose was twofold: to prevent warfare between the native Osage Indians and the Cherokees, who were new arrivals from the southern Appalachians; and to prevent white men from encroaching on Indian lands. The garrison was successful in keeping the peace, and in 1839 the Army abandoned it. In 1836, when Arkansas was admitted to the Union, the citizens demanded protection from possible Indian uprisings. Thus in 1839 the Army commenced building a new Fort Smith near the earlier one. But the frontier had already moved farther west, and the fort soon came to be used merely as a supply depot. During the Civil War Fort Smith served as a hospital. In 1872 the Federal Court for the Western District of Arkansas (which included 74,000 miles of Indian territory) established quarters in the former barracks building of Fort Smith. Here from 1875 until his death in 1896, the famous "Hanging Judge," Isaac C. Parker, presided over a court, keeping peace in the lawless territory. The only significant remains of the second fort are the old stone **Commissary Building** and **Judge Parker's Courtroom,** which has been restored.

For further information write: Box 1406, Fort Smith, AR 72902

PEA RIDGE NATIONAL MILITARY PARK, *11 miles northeast of Rogers, adjacent to U.S. 62*

Pea Ridge, just south of the Missouri border, was the site of the Federal victory that secured Missouri for the Union and influenced

the course of the Civil War throughout the Mississippi Valley. This park preserves the entire battlefield where, on March 7–8, 1862, this decisive Civil War action took place. Brigadier General Samuel R. Curtis, who was in charge of the Union mission to gain control of Missouri, began his campaign in southwestern Missouri late in December, 1861. By February 1862 Curtis's Federals had forced the Confederates of the Missouri state guard to retreat into Arkansas. By the end of the month the inadequate Confederate army had been enlarged with regular troops and was encamped in the Boston Mountains about midway between Fayetteville and Fort Smith *(see)*. On March 3 Major General Earl Van Dorn, grandnephew of Andrew Jackson, took command of the Confederate forces. Early in the day of March 7, 1862, 2 areas of battle developed: one near **Elkhorn Tavern**, the other 2 miles away near a little hamlet called **Leetown**. The 2 areas were separated by Round Top Mountain and other high ground. On the first day the Confederate army, which included an Indian brigade, won at Elkhorn Tavern but was decisively beaten at Leetown. The next day most of the fighting was in the tavern vicinity. A lack of ammunition forced most of the Confederates to retreat, and the Battle of Pea Ridge ended in overall Federal victory. The Confederates went to Van Buren, Arkansas, and after gathering their scattered forces they moved on into Tennessee, arriving too late to participate in the bloody Battle of Shiloh. Visitors can see the restored tavern and follow a self-guiding auto tour of the battlefield.
For further information write: Superintendent, Pea Ridge, AR 72751

CALIFORNIA

COLOMA NATIONAL HISTORIC LANDMARK, *7 miles northwest of Placerville on State 49*

At 7:30 a.m. on January 24, 1848, James Wilson Marshall came upon glittering particles in the tailrace of a sawmill belonging to John Sutter, on the south fork of the American River. Marshall exclaimed, "Boys, I believe I have found a gold mine!" Reports of this strike precipitated the California gold rush of 1848–49, when some 80,000 people flocked to the gold fields. The community of Coloma, which grew up around Marshall's discovery site, became known as the Queen of the Mines. Today visitors may see a replica of the sawmill, Marshall's wooden cabin, a historical museum, and ruins of many old structures.

DEATH VALLEY NATIONAL MONUMENT, *headquarters at Furnace Creek*

This great desert basin on the California-Nevada border received its present name from forty-niners who made a nearly disastrous trek across it on their way to the gold fields. Indians had occupied the valley for hundreds of years, as evidenced by the numerous petroglyphs, campsites, and foot trails found throughout the region. When the first covered wagons entered the valley on Christmas Day, 1849, the area was inhabited by the Panamint Indians. Although many pioneers nearly starved or died of thirst while crossing this inhospitable terrain, only one man actually perished. For decades prospectors flocked to Death Valley in search of silver or other metals. Death Valley's peak period occurred in the 1880s with the production of

borax, the "white gold of the desert," which was hauled out by the 20-mule-team trains of high-wheeled wagons. Today ghost towns like Skidoo are reminders of once-thriving mining communities.
For further information write: Superintendent, Death Valley, CA 92328

FORT ROSS NATIONAL HISTORIC LANDMARK, *13 miles north of Jenner on State 1*

In 1812 the Russian-American Company sent approximately 95 Russian and 40 Aleutian fur traders from Alaska to northern California. They erected a stockaded trading post and fort out of redwood on this small elevated coastal plateau at the site of a Pomo Indian village. For the next 29 years the Russians hunted fur seals and sea otters along the California coast and stored the pelts at Fort Ross before shipment to China, Manchuria, and European ports. In 1821 the Tsar's attempt to close the Pacific coast north of San Francisco to any but Russian ships precipitated a diplomatic controversy which resulted in that part of the Monroe Doctrine (of 1823) prohibiting Europeans from extending their holdings in the New World. By 1839 the Russians had virtually decimated the herds of fur seals and sea otters, and in 1841 they negotiated the sale of their outpost to Captain John A. Sutter for $30,000 in gold and produce. Within the present grounds, visitors may see the restored **Russian Orthodox Chapel,** stockade, blockhouse, and **Commander's House** (NHL), an outstanding and almost unaltered example of a Russian log house.

HEARST SAN SIMEON NATIONAL HISTORIC LANDMARK, *94 miles south of Monterey via State 1*

On a coastal knoll set against the Santa Lucia Mountains and overlooking the Pacific, publishing magnate William Randolph Hearst created La Cuesta Encantada (The Enchanted Hill), 123 acres of terraced gardens, pools, palatial guesthouses, and the fabled mansion **La Casa Grande.** Hearst built the estate in 1919 to house his immense collection of antiques and art.
Open daily 8–3:30

LOS ANGELES AND VICINITY

EL PUEBLO DE LOS ANGELES STATE HISTORIC PARK, *100 Calle de La Plaza*

In 1781 Governor Felipe de Neve, leading a party of Franciscan priests, 11 families, and a few soldiers, left the Mission San Gabriel to found the new community of El Pueblo de Nuestra Señora la Reina de Los Angeles. By 1800, 30 adobe houses and one church had grown up around a central plaza; a half century later the plaza was the heart of a thriving city. Much of the original Spanish town has been preserved or restored within this park. Today a bronze statue of Governor de Neve stands in the **Old Plaza.** The **Old Mission Church** nearby, the oldest religious edifice in the city, was founded by Franciscans in 1814, funded by proceeds from selling California brandy. On **Olvera Street,** a reconstruction of a typical Mexican village street, stands the **Avila Adobe,** built about 1818 by Don José María Avila, one-time mayor of the town; in 1847, after the Battle of Los Angeles, the house was occupied by Commodore Robert Stockton. Other points of interest include Pico House, an elegant 3-story hotel erected in 1869, and the **Old Plaza Firehouse** of 1884.

SACRAMENTO

OLD SACRAMENTO NATIONAL HISTORIC LANDMARK, *Sacramento Waterfront*

An outgrowth of the settlement established by Captain John A. Sutter in 1839 *(see Sutter's Fort National Historic Landmark)*, Sacramento emerged during the gold rush of 1848–49 as a major distribution point, serving the gold fields in the Sierra Nevada to the east and linking them with the coast on the west. Sacramento became the capital of the new state of California in 1854, and in subsequent years the transportation terminus for the first railroad in California (1856), the pony express (1860), river boat, telegraph, and the first transcontinental railroad. The original business district, now Old Sacramento, preserves a greater number of the park buildings—including banks, express buildings, hotels, restaurants, and stores—than any other major city on the Pacific coast.

SUTTER'S FORT NATIONAL HISTORIC LANDMARK, *2701 L Street*

Begun by Captain John Augustus Sutter in 1839 in order to protect an extensive land grant of some 72 square miles, this fort on the fork of the American and Sacramento rivers became an important outpost of civilization, providing shelter and supplies for weary travelers making their way west. In 1848 Sutter served as a delegate to the constitutional convention in Monterey that paved the way for California's admission as the 31st state. After the discovery of gold in 1848 at his sawmill in Coloma *(see Coloma Historic District)*, he retired to his farm on the Feather River. During the ensuing stampede for gold, Sutter's property passed out of his hands. Successive attempts to have Congress recognize his land claim proved futile, and Sutter died in poverty back east in 1880. The reconstructed fort and mining exhibits are preserved in a state historic park.

SAN DIEGO AND VICINITY

MISSION SAN DIEGO DE ALCALA NATIONAL HISTORIC LANDMARK, *7 miles north, in Mission Valley*

Founded on July 16, 1769, by Father Junípero Serra, San Diego de Alcalá was the "mother mission" of the chain of 21 missions. Originally situated on Presidio Hill in what is now Old Town San Diego *(see)*, the mission was relocated to its present site in 1774. The first irrigation system in California was developed at the mission, and the first palm and olive trees planted here.

OLD TOWN SAN DIEGO STATE HISTORIC PARK, *4016 Wallace Street*

For the first half century after its founding in 1769, life at San Diego had centered around its presidio *(see)* and the Mission San Diego de Alcalá *(see)*. Gradually, however, retired soldiers and their families began to settle on plots of land outside the presidio, and the community of Old Town began to develop. During the Mexican and well into the American period—The Stars and Stripes was raised on the plaza by Marines from the U.S.S. *Cyane* on July 29, 1846—ranches and rancheros flourished here, and Old Town became an international

According to his mistress, Marion Davies, William Randolph Hearst always called his grandiose, eclectic San Simeon estate "the ranch."

STATE OF CALIFORNIA, DEPARTMENT OF PUBLIC WORKS

center of the cowhide ("California banknote") and tallow trade. After the droughts of the 1860s and the development of a newer commercial district near the wharf, Old Town began to decline: a disastrous fire in 1872 dealt a death blow to the area as the heart of San Diego. Today 3 adobe buildings dating from 1827 to 1840 have been restored: **Casa de Estudillo** (NHL), **Casa de Machado y Stewart**, and **Casa Machado y Silvas**, which serves as park headquarters. Other buildings from the period include: **Casa de Bandini**, now a restaurant, the **Mason Street School**, and the **San Diego Union Building**, which has been restored to its 1868 appearance. There are also 2 reconstructed buildings: the **Racine and Laramie** store and the **Seeley Stable**, which houses a collection of horse-drawn vehicles and western memorabilia.
Open daily 10–5.

SAN DIEGO PRESIDIO NATIONAL HISTORIC LANDMARK, *Presidio Park*

Located on a hill in the historic heart of San Diego is the site of the first permanent Spanish settlement on the Pacific coast of California (1769). By 1835 the original structures had fallen into ruin, and in 1838 **Fort Stockton** was built on the site. In 1846 it became a U.S. Army post, and it was here in 1847 that the Mormon Battalion ended its march from Council Bluffs. One may still see fragments of the original fort's ramparts and the commemorative Father Serra Cross and Statue.

SAN FRANCISCO AND VICINITY

ALCATRAZ ISLAND, *San Francisco Bay*

This former Federal prison, built as a top-security installation, has had a long and varied history. The island, known as "the rock," is a part of **Golden Gate National Recreation** area with headquarters at Fort Mason. Alcatraz can be reached by ferry from Pier 41.
Ferries depart daily 8:45–2:45; hours extended in summer.

NATIONAL MARITIME MUSEUM, *Aquatic Park, foot of Polk Street*

Moored along a pier on San Francisco's historic waterfront, these carefully restored vessels constitute a fascinating display of nautical history on the Pacific coast. The collection includes the *C. A. Thayer* (NHL), a 3-masted schooner launched in 1895; the paddle-wheeled *Eureka* of 1890, which was the world's largest ferry; the *Alma*, a flat-bottomed, shallow-draft scow schooner built in 1891; the tugboat "Hercules"; and the side-wheel paddle-tug *Eppleton Hill*, an example of the earliest type of tugboat on the bay. Three blocks east of here at Fisherman's Wharf is the queen of the museum's fleet, the full-rigged sailing ship *Balclutha*, a veteran of 17 roundings of Cape Horn.
Ships open daily 10–5. Museum closed Mon; hours extended in summer.

SAN GABRIEL

MISSION SAN GABRIEL ARCANGEL, *Junípero Street and West Mission Drive*

Fathers Pedro Benito Cambón and Angel Fernández de la Somera established the San Gabriel mission in 1771. For nearly 50 years it served as the only outpost of civilization west of the vast California desert. Partially destroyed in an earthquake, the original church has been restored and boasts massive buttresses and bells. California's first winery was founded behind the mission. Today the oldest grapevine in the world—covering more than 12,000 square feet—grows on its ground.

SAN JUAN CAPISTRANO

MISSION SAN JUAN CAPISTRANO, *Camino Capistrano and Ortego Highway*

This mission has become internationally famous because of the flock of swallows that make their home here; the birds are supposed to arrive punctually every March 19 and depart on October 23. Father Junipero Serra founded California's seventh mission in 1776 and dedicated a small adobe church—now restored—at the site 2 years later. A stone church that was one of the largest and most elaborately decorated of the entire mission chain was constructed from 1797 to 1806, but the earthquake of 1812 caused the tower and heavy roof to come crashing down on the congregation. Today this structure is a picturesque ruin.

COLORADO

BENT'S OLD FORT NATIONAL HISTORIC SITE, *8 miles east of La Junta on State 194*

In 1830 Charles and William Bent and Ceran St. Vrain, upper Missouri River fur traders, formed a partnership to build a great trading establishment on the Arkansas River. They chose a spot on the north bank of the Arkansas about 12 miles west of the mouth of the Purgatoire River. This strategic location placed them just north of the New Mexico border in the heart of Indian country and on the mountain branch of the **Santa Fe Trail**, a key overland route. By 1833 the massive, impregnable mud fortress, now called Bent's Old Fort, became the hub of a trading empire that stretched from Texas into Wyoming, from the Rockies to middle Kansas. Bent's Fort was a significant fur-trading post, a rendezvous for trappers and Indians, a way station on the Santa Fe Trail, and the chief point of contact between the southern Plains Indians and the whites. During the Mexican War (1846–48) the fort became a supply base for the American conquest of New Mexico. After the war the Indian trade declined, and in 1849 William Bent abandoned the fort. Beginning in 1861 it was rehabilitated as the principal stop of the Barlow & Sanderson stage, mail, and express route between Kansas City and Santa Fe. The fort has now been completely reconstructed and refurnished to its appearance in 1846.
For further information write: 35110 Hwy. 194 E., La Junta, CO 81050

CRIPPLE CREEK HISTORIC DISTRICT NATIONAL HISTORIC LANDMARK, *State 67*

From the 1891 gold discovery by cowboy Bob Womack until the last mine closed in 1961, gold valued at more than $500 million was dug out of the hills of this district. Among the extant buildings to survive a 1906 blaze in this typical gold camp are the old headquarters of the **Western Federation of Mines**, the former **Midland Railroad Depot**, which now houses the Cripple Creek District Museum, and the 1896 **Imperial Hotel.**
Museum open: Memorial Day–mid-Oct, daily 10–5; rest of the year Sat, Sun 10–5

DENVER

BROWN PALACE HOTEL, *Tremont and Broadway at Seventeenth Street*

The Brown Palace, opened in 1892, was the brainchild of Henry C. Brown, a carpenter who came to Denver in 1860 and within three years was prosperous enough to buy 160 acres on hills east of the town—an area that he called Brown's Bluff and that would one day become the site of many great mansions built by Denver's silver and gold kings. Brown later began making plans to build an elegant Italian Renaissance-style hotel. The Brown Palace, one of the first fireproof buildings in America, took 5 years and $1.6 million to build and $400,000 to furnish.

LARIMER SQUARE, *1400 block of Larimer Street*

This square, part of Denver's Skyline Urban Renewal Project, reproduces the Denver of the 1860s, complete with a flea market, stores, galleries, and flower stalls. The square was the center of Denver's business life in the 19th century.

THE MOLLY BROWN HOUSE, *1340 Pennsylvania Street*

This Victorian house, situated in Denver's affluent Capitol Hill area, was built about 1890 and purchased in 1894 by Mr. and Mrs. James J. Brown. Mrs. Brown later became famous as the "Unsinkable Molly Brown" of the Broadway musical.

Open: Memorial Day-Labor Day, Mon-Sat 10–4, Sun 12–4; Apr-May, Sept, Tues-Sat 10–4, Sun 12–4; Oct-Mar, Tues-Sat 10–3, Sun 12–3

Potted palms and lounging men adorn the splendid, arched lobby of the Brown Palace Hotel at the turn of the century.

LIBRARY OF CONGRESS

STATE CAPITOL, *Capitol Hill, East Colfax and East Fourteenth avenues*
Construction on the 3-story granite capitol was started in 1890 and completed in 1907 at a cost of almost $3 million. The classical building is embellished with murals, portraits, statuary, and bronze doors that depict the history of the state.
Open: Mon-Fri 8–5; tours 10–3

UNITED STATES MINT, *300 block of West Colfax*
One of 3 Federal coinage plants in the nation, the Denver mint—which has been in operation since 1869—is a good repository.
Open: Mon-Fri 8:30–3

DURANGO-SILVERTON NARROW-GAUGE RAILROAD NATIONAL HISTORIC LANDMARK, *between Durango and Silverton, through San Juan National Forest*
Now part of the Denver and Rio Grande Western Railroad system, this narrow-gauge railroad was completed in 1882. The Silverton train was used to haul ores economically and efficiently from isolated mountain areas to points where smelters could operate. The train has been in continuous use since it was built. The typically Victorian coaches and locomotives, all vintage 1880s, now take tourists through magnificent Rocky Mountain scenery.
Operates daily weather permitting

GEORGETOWN-SILVER PLUME HISTORIC DISTRICT NATIONAL HISTORIC LANDMARK, *on I-70*
This region produced more than $90 million in gold, silver, lead, copper, and zinc between 1859 and 1939. Until the great silver strike at Leadville *(see)* began in 1878, Georgetown was the most productive silver camp in Colorado. The still-active communities of Silver Plume and Georgetown have retained much of their boom town atmosphere. The **Georgetown Loop Historic Mining Area** includes early mines and the famous **Georgetown Loop**, a narrow-gauge railroad once called the "Scenic Wonder of the West." A portion of the original 4.47 miles of track has been reconstructed and the trains operate in summer. The only major mining town never to have been ravaged by fire, Georgetown still has many 19th-century buildings. The **Hamill House** was the most luxurious dwelling in Colorado. The **Hotel de Paris** (1875), now a museum, was one of the most celebrated hotels west of the Mississippi.
Trains operate daily Memorial Day-Labor Day, 10:15–4:30 from Silver Plume and 11–4 from Georgetown. Mine tours optional.

LEADVILLE
LEADVILLE HISTORIC DISTRICT NATIONAL HISTORIC LANDMARK, *on U.S. 24 and State 91*
Leadville first became famous as a gold-mining area in 1860; later it became the silver capital of Colorado as well. It has been estimated that the district produced about $136 million in silver between 1879 and 1889. After the collapse of silver prices in 1893, Leadville miners once more concentrated on gold production, continuing to do so until the end of the century. Since then lead, zinc, manganese, and molybdenum have been mined in the district. The 9-mile highway of

the "Silver Kings" encircles the mining operations that made Leadville a leading ore producer. Many of the early structures have survived. These include the **Tabor House** (1877), built by the famous silver king H. A. W. Tabor and his wife, Augusta; the **Tabor Opera House** (1879); and the Victorian **Healy House (1878).**

MESA VERDE NATIONAL PARK, *southwest Colorado, southeast of Cortez*

This 52,000-acre park contains hundreds of spectacular cliff dwellings and mesa-top pit houses and pueblos inhabited by Indians from about the first century A.D. until almost 1300. Mesa Verde—the green table—was named by the Spaniards who first saw it in the 1700s. The earliest direct evidence of Indian habitation of what is now Mesa Verde occurred during the Modified Basket Maker Period (A.D. 400–700). During this time people built pit houses, which were shallow holes in the earth covered with sticks, on the mesa top, enabling them to live close to their crops. During the Developmental Pueblo Period (700–1000) the Indians constructed above-ground homes of stone and adobe, arranged in compact groups around open courts. During the Great, or Classic, Pueblo Period (A.D 1000–1300) the arts and crafts reached their peak. From about 1000 to about 1200 the Indians lived in well-constructed stone pueblos on the mesa top, with some houses reaching a height of four stories. About 1200, possibly because of raids by covetous nomads, the Indians retreated to the greater security of the cliff dwellings, great villages in caves at the heads of canyons, where living conditions were much more difficult than on the mesa top. Then in the 1270s the villages of Mesa Verde were abandoned, probably because of a severe drought that hit the whole region. Among the innumerable attractions here are the **Cliff Palace,** a village of more than 200 rooms and 23 kivas, **Far View House,** a large mesa-top pueblo, **Balcony House,** built into the wall of Soda Canyon, and **Fewkes Canyon Ruins,** a group of cliff dwellings. *For further information write: Superintendent, CO 81330*

PIKES PEAK NATIONAL HISTORIC LANDMARK, *15 miles west of Colorado Springs*

On November 23, 1806, on an expedition to determine the southwest boundary of the Louisiana Purchase, Lieutenant Zebulon M. Pike reached the present site of Pueblo. Pike and a few men then set out to climb the great peak that now bears Pike's name, but they failed to reach the summit. Set forward from the front range of the Rockies, Pikes Peak appears to rise much higher than its actual 14,110 feet. During the gold rush of 1859 it was the landmark that guided thousands of prospectors westward. Many of the Conestoga wagons that crossed the plains bore the inscription "Pikes Peak or Bust!" Pikes Peak was made accessible by the Manitou & Pikes Peak Railway, better known as the cog railway, which has been in operation since 1891.

CONNECTICUT

HARTFORD

NOOK FARM, *Farmington Avenue and Forest Street*

This remarkable neighborhood in the western section of Hartford, once inhabited by a group of interrelated friends and families, became something of a cultural center late in the 19th century, when

Epitomizing the simple elegance of New England churches, the Congregational Church in Litchfield gleams in autumn sunlight.

SAMUEL CHAMBERLAIN, MARBLEHEAD, MASS.

boasted such illustrious residents as Harriet Beecher Stowe and Mark Twain. The author of *Uncle Tom's Cabin* lived in a Victorian home built in 1870 for the last 23 years of her life. Mark Twain had a rambling Victorian-Gothic mansion (NHL) designed on one side in the shape of a river boat, where he lived from 1874 to 1879. The noteworthy interiors, designed by Louis C. Tiffany, have been restored.
Open: June-Aug, daily 10–4:30; Sept-May, Tues-Sat 9:30–4, Sun 1–4

LITCHFIELD HISTORIC DISTRICT NATIONAL HISTORIC LANDMARK
Serving as a trading center and outpost along Connecticut's northwestern frontier until late in the 18th century, Litchfield today with its central common and Revolutionary houses is one of the best preserved early "New England towns" in the state. Here in 1774 Judge Tapping Reeve founded America's first law school in a one-room building near his home. At classes conducted by Reeve and Judge James Gould in the **Tapping Reeve Law School** (NHL), young men were exposed to American common law in its formative stages. The school's illustrious alumni include 2 vice presidents —Aaron Burr and John C. Calhoun—3 members of the U.S. Supreme Court, 6 cabinet members, and more than 100 U.S. senators and congressmen.
Reeve House and school open: May 15-Oct 15, Thurs-Mon 12–4

MYSTIC

MYSTIC SEAPORT AND MUSEUM, *along the Mystic River on State 27*
One of the foremost maritime attractions in this country, Mystic Seaport preserves the authentic flavor of Connecticut's seafaring past. About 1850 Mystic's shipyards were producing the fastest clipper ships in the nation. And in 1861 the first regular ironclad vessel, the *Galena*, was fabricated at Mystic. Today the *Charles W. Morgan* (NHL), last of the 19th-century wooden whaleships, is permanently berthed here, as are the square-rigged mariner training ship *Joseph Conrad* and the Gloucester fishing schooner *L. A. Dunton*. Other features of this coastal village include a planetarium of celestial navigation and houses of the period.
Open: May-Oct, daily 9–5; Nov-Apr, daily 9–4

DELAWARE

NEW CASTLE

NEW CASTLE HISTORIC DISTRICT NATIONAL HISTORIC LANDMARK, *bordered by Harmony Street, The Strand, Third Street, and Delaware Street*
This unique example of a colonial capital has remained virtually unchanged since the early 19th century. Founded in 1651 as Fort Casimir by the Dutch, New Castle surrendered to the Swedes under Johan Rising in 1654, was retaken by the Dutch under Peter Stuyvesant in 1655 and renamed New Amstel, and was finally captured by the English in 1664, at which time it received its present name. William Penn, who was granted all the land within a 12-mile radius, arrived in New Castle in 1682. The town served as the capital of Delaware from 1704 until the Revolution. Today many fine town houses dating as far back as 1679 are preserved. On the third Saturday in May they are traditionally opened to the public.

WILMINGTON AND VICINITY

THE HAGLEY MUSEUM, *3 miles north on State 52, then 1 mile east*

Occupying a 185-acre tract along the Brandywine River on the site of the original powder works founded by Eleuthère Irénée Du Pont in 1802, this museum contains indoor and outdoor exhibits tracing American industrial development from colonial times to the present. About a mile away stands the stone residence **Eleutherian Mills** (NHL), erected in 1803 by Eleuthère Du Pont near the powder mills, so that labor and management would share the same danger from explosions. As early as 1810 Du Pont's powder mill complex was the largest factory in the nation; it supplied American forces with gunpowder during the War of 1812. After 1860, E. I. Du Pont de Nemours & Company began to diversify its interests. Today the company is primarily a manufacturer of chemicals and is one of the nation's major industries. The main exhibit building is an 1814 textile mill that was converted to the manufacture of powder kegs.

Apr-Dec, daily 9:30–4; Jan-Mar, Sat, Sun 9:30–4:30, guided tour weekdays at 1:30

HENRY FRANCIS DU PONT WINTERTHUR MUSEUM, *6 miles northwest on State 52*

This museum houses the richest and most extensive collection of early American interior architecture, furniture, and decorative accessories ever assembled. Nearly 200 period rooms provide a vivid record of the American domestic scene between the years 1640 and 1840. Erected in 1839, Winterthur was named after the town in Switzerland whence its owners, Mr. and Mrs. J. A. Biderman, had emigrated. Their grandnephew, Henry Francis Du Pont, developed the 60-acre gardens over a period of about 50 years, and in 1927 began to acquire his famous collection.

Write for tour information: Winterthur Reservations Office, Winterthur, DE 19735

DISTRICT OF COLUMBIA

CONGRESSIONAL CEMETERY, *1801 E Street, SE*

Since 1817, when 100 burial sites were set aside for use by the Federal government, many legislators and executive officials who died in the Capital have been buried here. To date 14 senators and 43 representatives are interred in this cemetery, along with such other notables as Vice President Elbridge Gerry, John Philip Sousa, Mathew Brady, and Sioux chief Scarlet Crow.

DECATUR HOUSE NATIONAL HISTORIC LANDMARK, *748 Jackson Place, NW*

Commodore Stephen Decatur, naval hero of the Tripolitan war and the War of 1812, lived in this house designed for him by Benjamin Latrobe for the last 14 months of his life. Famous for having said, "Our country may she always be in the right; but our country, right or wrong," Decatur was killed in a duel by Captain James Barron, an old and bitter enemy. Subsequent residents of this lovely brick mansion include Henry Clay, Martin Van Buren, and Judah Benjamin. The restored house displays Decatur memorabilia.

Open: Tues-Fri 10–2, Sat, Sun 12–4

DUMBARTON OAKS, *1703 32nd Street, NW*
In 1944 representatives of the United States, Great Britain, the Soviet Union, and China met in this stately Georgian mansion to discuss a permanent postwar international organization. The agreements reached here, known as the Dumbarton Oaks Plan, served as the basis of the United Nations Charter. Today the mansion houses Harvard University's Center for Byzantine Studies, featuring formal gardens, an extensive library, and a pre-Columbian art collection.
House open: Nov–Mar, daily 2–5; gardens daily: Apr–Oct, 2–6; Nov–Mar, 2–5

FORD'S THEATRE NATIONAL HISTORIC SITE, *511 Tenth Street, NW*
With the stage set for the second scene of the third act of *Our American Cousin*, Ford's Theatre looks almost exactly as it did on April 14, 1865, when shortly after 10 p.m. John Wilkes Booth crept into the presidential box and shot Abraham Lincoln. Built by John T. Ford in 1863, the theater was closed following the assassination. Attempts to reopen it in June met with such public outrage that the government took over the building. Not until 1968, when the present restoration was completed, was the building again open to the public as a theater. An outstanding museum of Lincolniana is housed in the basement.
Museum open daily 9–5

FREDERICK DOUGLASS HOME, *1411 W Street, SE*
"Do not judge me by the heights to which I have risen," said slave-born Frederick Douglass, "but by the depths from which I have come." The self-educated son of a slave mother and an unknown white father, Douglass fled north in 1838 and rose to become, in Lincoln's words, "one of the most meritorious men . . . in the United States." As lecturer, author, and editor-publisher of the *North Star*, Douglass was one of the nation's leading abolitionist spokesmen. After the Civil War, for which he raised Negro troops, he served in a variety of government posts including marshal for the District of Columbia and minister to Haiti. Douglass lived here at Cedar Hill from 1879 until his death in 1895; today the restored house and museum are preserved as a memorial to him.
Open: Apr–Aug, daily 9–5; Sept–Mar, daily 9–4

GEORGETOWN HISTORIC DISTRICT NATIONAL HISTORIC LANDMARK
Laid out in 1751 and incorporated as an independent town in the District of Columbia in 1789, this quaint area was the hub of social and diplomatic life in the early days of the Republic. It was annexed to the city of Washington in 1878 and today still retains its early 19th-century charm. Although many of the beautiful town houses and public buildings predate the Revolution (among them the **Old Stone House**, built in 1765), most were constructed after 1800.

HOUSE WHERE LINCOLN DIED, *516 Tenth Street, NW*
After Abraham Lincoln was shot by John Wilkes Booth at Ford's Theatre *(see)* on the night of April 14, 1865, the President was moved across the street to William Petersen's home. Here in the small back bedroom on the first floor Lincoln died at 7:22 a.m., April 15. The

The Civil War stopped construction of the U.S. Capitol for a time. The familiar dome was not completed until 1863.
LIBRARY OF CONGRESS

modest home was purchased by the government in 1896 and was subsequently restored to its appearance on that fateful day.
Open daily 9–5

PENNSYLVANIA AVENUE NATIONAL HISTORICAL SITE

Pierre L'Enfant, designer of Washington, D.C., planned Pennsylvania Avenue as the shortest distance between the White House and the United States Capitol *(see both)*. Since 1791, when it was laid out, the avenue has been a ceremonial route for presidential inaugurations, 6 presidential funeral processions (including Lincoln's and Kennedy's), wartime victory celebrations, and various public and official demonstrations. Included in the historical site are the **Federal Triangle, Judiciary Square**, and sections of the commercial district of Washington.

PHILADELPHIA NATIONAL HISTORIC LANDMARK, *Smithsonian Institution, Fourteenth Street and Constitution Avenue, NW*

The only surviving gunboat built and manned by Americans during the Revolutionary War, the *Philadelphia* was raised from the bottom of Valcour Bay, a channel in Lake Champlain, in 1935. She had gone down there on October 11, 1776, during a 7-hour battle in which Benedict Arnold's fleet of 16 small boats was severely defeated by a superior British force under Sir Guy Carleton. Preserved by the cold waters of the bay, the *Philadelphia* is now on display in the Smithsonian National Museum of American History.
Open daily 10–5:30; hours extended in summer

SMITHSONIAN INSTITUTION

Established in 1846 with money willed by James Smithson, the illegitimate son of the first Duke of Northumberland, the Smithsonian has grown to include a vast complex of museums, art galleries, and research facilities constituting one of the most extensive collections in the world. Among the components of the Institution are the National Museum of American History, the National Air and Space Museum, the National Gallery of Art, the Museum of Natural History, the Museum of American Art, and the National Portrait Gallery. Within this complex one can see the original "Star-Spangled Banner," the Revolutionary War gunboat *Philadelphia (see)*, an outstanding collection of gowns belonging to the nation's First Ladies, Charles Lindbergh's *Spirit of St. Louis*, and John Glenn's *Friendship* 7. The famous original reddish-brown building, a National Historic Landmark, now houses administration offices and Smithson's tomb.
Open daily 10–5:30; hours extended in summer

UNITED STATES CAPITOL NATIONAL HISTORIC LANDMARK

Symbol of the nation and seat of the Congress, the Capitol was officially begun when George Washington laid the cornerstone on September 18, 1793. The building was based on Dr. William Thornton's design, revised by Benjamin Latrobe. Construction continued under a number of architects, and the famous domed structure topped by the bronze statue *Freedom* was not completed until 1906. Another addition was begun in 1958. The Senate occupies the north wing of the Capitol, and the House of Representatives the south. Until 1935 the Supreme Court also held sessions here. From the

Court's old basement office Samuel F. B. Morse sent out the world's first telegraph message in 1844. Since 1817, when James Monroe became Chief Executive, official presidential inaugurations have been held outside the east front of the Capitol, where a temporary platform is constructed for the swearing-in.
Open: Sept–May, daily 9–4:30; June–Aug, daily 9–10

THE WHITE HOUSE, *1600 Pennsylvania Avenue*
In 1792 George Washington laid the cornerstone at the mansion that has been the home of every American President except him. Designed by James Hoban on a site selected by Washington himself, the 132-room White House is today much larger than it was in 1800 when John Adams moved in. Burned by the British in 1814, the "President's Palace" was not occupied again until 1817, when new white paint applied to the exterior walls gave it its present name. From 1948 to 1952 the White House underwent extensive renovation. (During this time President Truman and his family lived in the historic **Blair House** across the street.) Under Mrs. John F. Kennedy the Executive Mansion was redecorated with authentic furnishings of historical importance. Among the rooms open to the public are the **State Dining Room**, which can accommodate 140 guests; the **Blue Room**, furnished in the period of James Monroe's administration; and the **East Room**, where Nellie Grant, Alice Roosevelt, and Lynda Bird Johnson were married. On display in the East Room is Gilbert Stuart's famous portrait of George Washington, which Dolley Madison saved from the British.
Open Tues–Sat 10–12; Special congressional tours, Tues–Sat 8:15, 8:30, 8:45, contact local congressperson

FLORIDA

CAPE CANAVERAL AIR FORCE STATION AND JOHN F. KENNEDY SPACE CENTER, *across Indian River from U.S. 1 between Titusville and Cocoa*
The Cape Canaveral Air Force Station has been the launching site of U.S. manned flights since May 5, 1961, when Navy Commander Alan B. Shepard, Jr., was hurled about 115 miles into outer space in *Freedom VII*, his Project Mercury capsule. Since then over 2,000 missiles have been blasted into space from Cape Canaveral. The Cape Canaveral Air Force Station, which is east of the space center across the Banana River, serves both as the actual launching site and as a development and testing center for military and NASA missile systems. NASA offers daily (except Christmas and major launching days) two escorted bus tours of the space center and Air Force Station. The tour of the space center includes a visit to the Astronaut Training building, where one can see a full-scale model of an astronaut lowering his lunar rover from the lunar module on the moon's surface. The tour passes Pad A, from which the Space Shuttle is launched, and the Vehicle Assembly Building, which features a full-sized model of the Saturn V rocket. The tour of the Air Force Station includes a visit to the Air Force Space Museum, where there is a remarkable collection of rockets on display. Both tours originate at **Spaceport, USA**, the outstanding visitor's center which features the IMAX/Galexy theaters and other exhibits about space.

FLORIDA KEYS AND VICINITY

FORT JEFFERSON NATIONAL MEMORIAL, *Dry Tortugas Island, 68 miles west of Key West in Gulf of Mexico*

Fort Jefferson was the largest of the chain of seacoast defenses built from Maine to Texas in the first half of the 19th century. The fort, once the key to control of the Gulf of Mexico, is the main attraction of the 7 Dry Tortugas Islands and the surrounding shoals and waters of the Gulf of Mexico, all of which are included in this 90-square-mile national monument. The Dry Tortugas are a cluster of coral keys that form the southwest tip of Florida Reef. In 1513 explorer Ponce de León named them "las Tortugas"—the Turtles—because of the large number of turtles breeding in the area. The U.S. Army began constructing Fort Jefferson in 1846, and although work continued for almost 30 years, the fort was never actually completed. Surrounded by a moat, this 6-sided brick fort covers most of 16-acre Garden Key. Its 8-foot-thick walls are 50 feet high, and its massive foundations rest on coral rock and sand 10 feet below sea level. The fort, built to garrison 1,500 men, has 3 gun tiers designed to hold 450 cannon. In January 1861, unarmed, half-completed Fort Jefferson was occupied by Federal troops to keep it from falling into the hands of Florida secessionists. After 1865, by which time it was militarily obsolete, the fort was used as a prison. Its inmates included several of the men accused of plotting Lincoln's assassination. In the 20th century fires and hurricanes turned the fort into a ruin. The monument may be reached by boat or seaplane from Key West *(see).*

For further information write: U.S. Coast Guard Base, Key West, FL 33040

KEY WEST, *about 130 miles south southwest of Miami via U.S. 1*

Key West, the southernmost city of the continental United States, is a tiny island city about 3 miles wide and 5 miles long. It lies at the end of the treacherous Florida Reef and is strategically situated between the Gulf of Mexico and the Atlantic Ocean. Key West was sighted in 1513 by Ponce de León when he sailed along the Florida Keys. The island's first owner was a Spanish cavalry officer who in 1821 sold it to John Simonton, an Alabama businessman. Key West began its rise to prominence as an international harbor and wrecking depot in the 1820s, when a U.S. naval base was established there. In 1831 Army barracks were built at Key West, and in 1845 construction began on **Fort Zachary Taylor** (recently designated a national monument), built as part of the United States coastal defense system. Key West was the only southern town to remain in Union hands throughout the Civil War. In 1912 Key West became the terminus for the railroad linking Miami and Key West. Built by Henry Flagler, this railroad was destroyed by the hurricane that devastated Key West in 1935. The town remained isolated until 1938, when the 122-mile-long Overseas Highway (a section of U.S. 1) was completed between Florida City and Key West. Key West was a vital military and naval base in both world wars. The **Key West Historic District** includes the **Audubon House,** where John James Audubon lived in 1832 while painting Florida wildlife, and the **Ernest Hemingway House and Museum** (NHL), where the Pulitzer Prize-winning author lived from 1931 until his death in 1961. The **East and West Martello Towers,** both open to the public, are old Civil War forts built in 1861.

This aerial view of St. Augustine's Castillo de San Marcos makes it clear why the massive fortress was never breached.

ST. AUGUSTINE AND ST. JOHNS COUNTY CHAMBER OF COMMERCE

ST. AUGUSTINE AND VICINITY

CASTILLO DE SAN MARCOS NATIONAL MONUMENT, *1 Castillo Drive; access via U.S. 1 and State A1A*

The northernmost outpost of Spain's New World empire, this great fortress was built between 1672 and 1696 to protect St. Augustine. The impregnable castillo is a symmetrical 4-sided building surrounded by a 40-foot-wide moat. It is the oldest masonry fortification in the United States; its 30-foot-high sloping walls, which are 16 feet wide at the base, are made of native shellstone called coquina, with mortar made from shell limestone. The castillo's baptism by fire occurred in 1702, during Queen Anne's War, when the British colonists of South Carolina burned St. Augustine and unsuccessfully besieged the fort. In 1740, during the War of Jenkins' Ear, General James Oglethorpe of Georgia captured and burned St. Augustine, but failed to take the castillo after a long siege. The fortress was also the target of raids by pirates and Indians, and the base from which the Spanish made several forays (1686, 1706, 1742) into the Carolinas and Georgia. The castillo was garrisoned by the British when they controlled Florida (1763–83). After Florida passed to the United States in 1821, the U.S. Army renamed the castillo Fort Marion in honor of the Revolutionary War hero Francis Marion. It was used as a prison, notably for Indians during the Second Seminole War, and during the Civil War Confederate forces occupied the fort briefly until Federal troops took it in 1862. During the Spanish-American War (1898), ironically, it served as a prison for Spanish soldiers.

For further information write: 1 Castillo Dr., St. Augustine, FL 32084

GEORGIA

ANDERSONVILLE NATIONAL HISTORIC SITE, *¼ mile east of Andersonville on State 49*

This historic site contains **Andersonville Prison** (formerly named Camp Sumter), where nearly 13,000 Union soldiers died between February 1864, and April 1865. In August 1864 nearly 33,000 Federals were imprisoned in the 26-acre stockade; heat, crowding, and disease took their grim toll. The inner-stockade commander, Captain Henry Wirz, was the only Confederate official to be executed by the Federal government for war crimes. However, witnesses had testified that Wirz was not personally responsible, and he was posthumously exonerated from charges of cruelty. Visitors can see unfinished escape tunnels made by the inmates as well as the site of the stockade and the surrounding fortifications. This national historic site also contains a national cemetery, the burial place of the Union soldiers who died while imprisoned at Andersonville.

For further information write: Superintendent, Andersonville, GA 31711

ATLANTA AND VICINITY

CYCLORAMA OF THE BATTLE OF ATLANTA, *at Park Avenue and the Boulevard*

The Cyclorama Building in Grant Park contains a huge painting —50 feet high and 400 feet long— that depicts the famous Battle of Atlanta, on July 22, 1864. The battle, the culmination of the Atlanta campaign, came 2 days after the Battle of Peachtree Creek, in which General William Tecumseh Sherman's Federals had successfully moved closer to Atlanta, rail hub and manufacturing center

In the bloody Civil War battle for Atlanta, Sherman's men almost leveled the city's roundhouse, as shown in this 1864 photograph.

ASSOCIATION OF AMERICAN RAILROADS TRANSPORTATION BUILDING, WASHINGTON, D.C.

of the Confederacy. Although the city was protected by 12 miles of earthworks, entrenchments, and gun emplacements, it could not hold out against the Union army. At the Battle of Atlanta some 4,000 Federals and 8,000 Confederates lost their lives. Atlanta subsequently remained under siege while Sherman captured the vital railroad lines in and out of the city, cutting Atlanta off from supplies and reinforcements. On September 2 Atlanta surrendered to Sherman, who evacuated the city and set fire to it on November 14, just before he began his destructive March to the Sea. Grant Park also contains **Old Fort Walker**, a Confederate battery built in 1864, and some Civil War breastworks.
Open daily 9:30–4:30

STONE MOUNTAIN PARK, *just east of I-285*
This historical park is noted for the colossal equestrian sculpture of Generals Robert E. Lee and Stonewall Jackson and Jefferson Davis carved into the granite wall of massive Stone Mountain. An antebellum plantation, a main house with period funishings and dependencies, has been reassembled here from other Georgia locations.
Open daily: summer 10–9, rest of year 10–5:30

DAHLONEGA

DAHLONEGA COURTHOUSE GOLD MUSEUM, *in Old Lumpkin County Courthouse, Public Square*
This museum commemorates the nation's first gold rush, which occurred in 1829 in northeast Georgia. The region was then Cherokee Territory, and the Indians regarded the hordes of prospectors who streamed across their land as intruders. The Cherokees had refused to sell their land in north Georgia to the United States; however, in 1830 the state of Georgia assumed ownership of gold-yielding Cherokee Territory, calling it Cherokee County. When Cherokee County was later divided into 10 smaller counties, the gold-discovery area became Lumpkin County. Dahlonega, from a Cherokee phrase meaning "place of yellow metal," was made the seat of Lumpkin County in 1833. A branch of the U.S. mint that operated from Dahlonega from 1838 to 1861 coined more than $6 million worth of Georgia gold. The dome of the state capitol in Atlanta is gilded with Lumpkin County gold.
Museum open: Tues–Sat 9–5, Sun 2–5:30

SAVANNAH AND VICINITY

FORT PULASKI NATIONAL MONUMENT, *17 miles east via U.S. 80*
Built between 1829 and 1847 on Cockspur Island as part of the chain of coastal defenses constructed in the first half of the 19th century, supposedly impregnable Fort Pulaski was the pride of Savannah. The fort was named after Casimir Pulaski, a hero of the Revolution *(see Savannah Historic District)*. After Georgia's secession it was occupied by Confederate forces. On April 11, 1862, Union rifled cannon forced the surrender of the fort, demonstrating for the first time that old-style masonry fortifications were ineffective against modern weapons. The capture of Fort Pulaski, strategically located at the mouth of the Savannah River, cut Savannah's access to foreign trade and tightened the hold of the Union naval blockade on the South's economic life. The **John Wesley Memorial** honors a missionary to the Indians who arrived at the island on February 5, 1736.
For further information write: Box 98, Tybee Island, GA 31328

SAVANNAH HISTORIC DISTRICT NATIONAL HISTORIC LANDMARK, *bounded by Bay, East Broad, Gwinnett, and West Broad streets*

This significant area of Georgia's colonial capital reflects much of the original plan devised by Savannah's founder, James Oglethorpe. Here he established the first settlement in Georgia, in February, 1733, as a debtors' colony. Laid out on a grand scale, with broad avenues and many open squares, Savannah was one of the first planned cities in North America. Of the 24 squares in the original plan, 5 are on Bull Street, within the historic district. During the Revolutionary War Savannah, with its strategic harbor, was an important target. The city was garrisoned by some 1,000 men under Patriot General Robert Howe when a superior British force captured it in 1778. In October 1779 an unsuccessful Franco-American attempt to retake Savannah resulted in the loss of about 800 men, including the Polish-born Revolutionary War hero Casimir Pulaski. In 1782, after their defeat at Yorktown, Virginia, the British evacuated Savannah and the war was over in Georgia. Few of Savannah's colonial structures survived the fire of 1796. The district preserves many Regency buildings of merit, notably those built between 1816 and 1825 by the English architect William Jay.

WARM SPRINGS

LITTLE WHITE HOUSE, *off U.S. 27A*

Built by President Franklin Delano Roosevelt in 1932 and used as his presidential retreat, the Little White House remains substantially as it was when he died there on April 12, 1945.

Open: Sept–May, Tues–Sun 9–5; June–Aug, Tues–Sun 9–6

HAWAII

ISLAND OF OAHU

HONOLULU AND VICINITY

IOLANI PALACE NATIONAL HISTORIC LANDMARK, *364 South King Street*

The only royal palace in the United States, this structure housed Hawaii's last 2 monarchs and also served as the seat of authority for the provisional government, the republic, the territory, and the state of Hawaii. Legislative sessions were held at the palace from 1895 until 1968, the house meeting in the throne room, and the senate convening in the dining room. Replacing an earlier palace built in 1845, the current Iolani Palace was constructed from 1879 to 1882 as a residence for King Kalakaua. After his death in 1891, Queen Liliuokalani occupied the premises. The ceremony formally transferring the sovereignty of the Hawaiian Islands to the United States took place on the palace steps on August 12, 1898.

Open for tours: Wed–Sat 9–2 by appointment

MISSION HOUSES AND KAWAIAHAO CHURCH NATIONAL HISTORIC LANDMARK, *King and Kawaiahao streets*

These buildings commemorate the first contingent of Protestant missionaries who arrived from New England in 1820 and in subsequent years strongly influenced the religion, education, medical practices, and economics of the Hawaiians. Built in 1821 of timbers from New England, the **Frame House** is the oldest structure of its

kind on the islands. A **Printing House** was erected in 1823 to house the Ramage press—a replica of which operates today—which struck off the first printing on Hawaii. The **Levi Chamberlain House** of 1831 was a home and also a depository for mission supplies. The Reverend Hiram Bingham dedicated his Congregational **Kawaiahao Church** in 1842. In Honolulu's oldest house of worship, King Kamehameha III is believed to have uttered, "The life of the land is perpetuated in righteousness," which has since become Hawaii's motto.
Open: Mon–Fri 9:30–12

USS ARIZONA MEMORIAL, PEARL HARBOR, *3 miles south of Pearl City on State 73*

On December 7, 1941, at the naval base at Pearl Harbor (NHL), Japan conducted the surprise air attack that precipitated the United States' entry into World War II. The battleship U.S.S. *Arizona* was sunk that day with 1,102 sailors trapped within, and the U.S.S. *Utah* went down with 58 men on board. Today the remains of the *Arizona* serve as a memorial to those who lost their lives.

IDAHO

NEZ PERCE NATIONAL HISTORICAL PARK, *northern Idaho, within an area 10–50 miles east of Lewiston via U.S. 12*

This vast stretch of country, encompassing 12,000 square miles, preserves and interprets the history and culture of the Nez Perce Indians and that of the white men—fur traders, missionaries, miners, and soldiers—who eventually engulfed and defeated them. In 1805 Meriwether Lewis and William Clark, on their expedition to the

On December 7, 1941, the U.S.S.* West Virginia *burns out of control after being smashed by Japanese bombs at Pearl Harbor.

U.S. NAVY PHOTOGRAPH, LIBRARY OF CONGRESS

Pacific, became the first explorers to encounter the Nez Perce, whom they found to be "among the most amiable men we have seen." For the next half century the Nez Perce maintained friendly relations with white settlers in the region. With the discovery of gold in Idaho in 1860, the U.S. government negotiated a treaty with the Indians, appropriating many of their lands and establishing reservations. Some of the Nez Perce people refused to recognize the legality of the treaty and to move off their traditional homeland. Tension and conflicts surrounding efforts to force these Indians onto the reservation erupted into the Nez Perce War of 1877. Today 24 widely scattered and dissimilar sites within the park commemorate this significant chapter in the annals of the Northwest. Important sites include (in order of their accessibility driving eastward from Lewiston on U.S. 95, and returning via State 13 and U.S. 12) **Fort Lapwai**, erected by Army volunteers in 1862 to promote harmonious relations between settlers and Indians on the newly created reservations. At **White Bird Battlefield**, on June 17, 1877, the Nez Perce routed a contingent of U.S. soldiers in the opening engagement of the Nez Perce War. A month later **Clearwater Battlefield** was the scene of a clash between the Indians and the Army, which ended in a draw. Lewis and Clark were introduced to the Nez Perce tribe at **Weippe Prairie** (NHL) on the western side of the Bitterroot Range. Idaho's first major gold discovery occurred at the town of **Pierce** in 1860. And the **Lolo Trail** (NHL) **and Pass**, originally an Indian path leading over the Bitterroot Mountains to buffalo country in Montana, were used by Lewis and Clark on their westward journey. During the Nez Perce War the trail provided an escape route for some 700 Indians who were being pursued by U.S. troops.
For further information write: Box 93, Spalding, ID 83551

ILLINOIS

CHICAGO AND VICINITY

HULL HOUSE NATIONAL HISTORIC LANDMARK, *800 South Halsted Street*

Jane Addams, pioneer social worker, founded this settlement house in 1889 in the slums of Chicago. Here she provided the poor with a variety of social services. She later became the first American woman to receive the Nobel Peace Prize.
Open: summer, Mon–Fri 10–4, Sun 12–5; rest of the year closed Sun

OLD WATER TOWER, *Michigan and Chicago avenues*

This landmark is one of the few survivors of the Great Chicago Fire of 1871, which almost destroyed the entire city.

PULLMAN HISTORIC DISTRICT NATIONAL HISTORIC LANDMARK, *east of Cottage Grove Avenue between 103rd and 115th streets*

During the 1880s George M. Pullman, inventor and manufacturer of the Pullman sleeping car, had this model settlement built for his employees. In 1894 the Illinois supreme court declared the company-sponsored housing project illegal, and the dwellings were sold to private owners. Many of the old structures stand today.

SITE OF FIRST SELF-SUSTAINING NUCLEAR REACTION NATIONAL HISTORIC LANDMARK, *South Ellis Avenue between East 56th and 57th streets*

On December 2, 1942, scientists, headed by the Italian-born physicist Enrico Fermi, produced the world's first self-sustaining nuclear chain reaction here in a converted squash-rackets court beneath the west stands of Stagg Field.

EAST ST. LOUIS

CAHOKIA MOUNDS NATIONAL HISTORIC LANDMARK, *east on U.S. 40*

The remains of the largest prehistoric Indian town—representing the fountainhead of Mississippian culture—in the United States have been uncovered at this site. From 50,000 to 60,000 dwellings were built here between A.D. 600 and A.D. 1400. Nearly 100 earthen mounds, used as platforms for rulers' houses or as mortuary temples, were constructed at Cahokia. **Monks' Mound**, a burial mound 1,037 feet long, 790 feet wide, and 100 feet high, is the largest in the nation and is a state historic site.

EADS BRIDGE. *See* ST. LOUIS, MISSOURI

GALENA HISTORIC DISTRICT

This once-important river-boat town on the Galena River preserves many fine examples of architecture built when Galena was the wealthiest city of Illinois in the mid–1800s. Historic structures include the **Market House**, formerly the hub of agricultural activities; the **John Dowling House**, erected in 1825 and the oldest residence in Galena; and a replica of the **J. R. Grant Leather Store**, where Ulysses S. Grant clerked for his father in 1860. Galena gave 9 generals, including Grant, to the Union army during the Civil War. Afterward the citizens of Galena presented Grant with a house as a token of their gratitude. Today the restored **Grant House** (NHL) contains family memorabilia.

Grant House and Market House State Memorials open daily 9–5. Grant Leather Store and Dowling House open: May–Oct, daily 9–4

NAUVOO HISTORIC DISTRICT NATIONAL HISTORIC LANDMARK

From 1839 until 1846 Nauvoo flourished as headquarters for the Church of the Latter Day Saints and principal settlement of the Mormons. Having fled religious persecution in Missouri, the Mormons, led by the church's founder, Joseph Smith, came to Illinois, where they established the community of Nauvoo. The town grew rapidly and within a few years boasted a population of 20,000. In 1841 Smith laid the foundation of a great temple, which was never completed because of his assassination, in 1844, by an angry mob in nearby Carthage. This structure was later destroyed. Illinois authorities became increasingly hostile toward the Mormons, whom they suspected of harboring criminals in their town. In 1846 the Mormons were expelled from the state. Led by Brigham Young, Smith's successor and the church's greatest colonizer, the Mormons began the trek that took them to the Valley of the Great Salt Lake in Utah. Nauvoo, from 1849 until 1858, was occupied by the Icarians, a communistic sect comprised of Frenchmen and Germans. Today only

Abraham Lincoln had his law office in the next-to-last building at right on this Springfield street, photographed in 1868.

LIBRARY OF CONGRESS

such fragments as the sunstone in Nauvoo State Park remain of the temple. Among the original Mormon buildings that still stand are the **Joseph Smith Homestead**, the **Mansion House** (Smith's second Illinois residence), the **Brigham Young House**, and the **Time and Seasons Buildings**, which housed the church printing office.
Houses open daily

SPRINGFIELD AND VICINITY

LINCOLN HOME NATIONAL HISTORICAL SITE, *Eighth and Jackson streets*

Abraham Lincoln resided in this simple frame house—the only home he ever owned—during the crucial years from 1844 to 1861, when he rose from a small-town lawyer to the Presidency of the United States. It was in the north parlor that Lincoln, on May 17, 1860, received the committee informing him of his nomination as the Republican presidential candidate. Lincoln also held a grand public levee here to bid good-by to the well-wishers before departing for Washington, D.C., in February 1861.
Open daily 8–5

LINCOLN TOMB STATE MEMORIAL, *Oak Ridge Cemetery*

This monument contains the tombs of Abraham Lincoln, Mary Todd Lincoln, and 3 of their 4 sons. Soon after Lincoln's assassination on April 14, 1865, the citizens of Springfield raised funds for a memorial to the martyred President. Larkin G. Mead, Jr., designed the monument, which was dedicated in 1874.
Open daily 9–5

LINCOLN'S NEW SALEM STATE HISTORIC SITE, *about 20 miles northwest off State 97*

While living in this village from 1831 to 1837, Abraham Lincoln embarked on his career of law and statesmanship. During his residence here, Lincoln enlisted in the Black Hawk War and was elected to the Illinois general assembly in 1834. Today New Salem has been authentically reconstructed; the only old structure remaining is the **Onstot Cooper Shop**, where young Lincoln studied by firelight.
Open daily 9–5

OLD STATE CAPITAL NATIONAL HISTORIC LANDMARK, *Adams Street*

The political careers of Abraham Lincoln, Stephen A. Douglas, and Ulysses S. Grant are linked to the Sangamon County Courthouse, which was begun in 1837 and served as Illinois' fifth State House until 1869. Lincoln sat in the state legislature here from 1840 to 1841; in 1858 he accepted the Republican nomination for the U.S. Senate and made his famous "House Divided" speech in the structure. Lincoln's political rival Douglas debated here during the 1858 Senate campaign and in 1861 made his famous address urging citizens to rally behind the Union. Grant served in the State House in 1861 as Illinois adjutant general.
Open Apr–Oct, Mon–Sat 8:30–5; Nov–Mar, Mon–Fri 8:30–5

INDIANA

NEW HARMONY HISTORIC DISTRICT NATIONAL HISTORIC LANDMARK

New Harmony was the home of two ambitious but short-lived 19th-century experiments in communal living. In 1815 Father George Rapp, a Lutheran Church dissenter, led his followers from Pennsylvania to Indiana, where he founded the village of Harmonie. The Rappites believed in community ownership, anticipated the second coming of Christ, and practiced celibacy in preparation. Urged on by their demanding leader, the hard-working, rigidly disciplined colonists in 10 years turned a wilderness into a thriving, self-sufficient community. Despite the community's success, in 1825 Rapp decided to return to Pennsylvania. Harmonie was purchased by Welsh philanthropist Robert Owen, who was eager to establish a utopian community. Scottish philanthropist William Maclure, who joined Owen, was particularly interested in education, and soon a distinguished group of educators and scientists gathered there. The colony established the first kindergarten in the United States, the first trade school, and the first free public school system. However, by 1827 the experiment had failed, probably because the colony lacked competent farmers and businessmen.

IOWA

AMANA VILLAGES NATIONAL HISTORIC LANDMARK, *20 miles west of Iowa City and 20 miles southwest of Cedar Rapids*

This was the most successful of the utopian communities that flourished in the United States in the middle years of the 19th century. An outgrowth of a German religious group who called themselves the Inspirationists, the sect immigrated to America after 1842, settled first in Ebenezer, New York, and then moved to Iowa in 1855, where they founded the village of Amana (the biblical term for "remain faithful"). The Amana Society subsequently established 5 other villages "one hour by oxen" apart and purchased the town of Homestead in 1861, where such houses as the **Amana Heim**, with its original furnishings, provide an authentic view of life in the Amana colony.

KANSAS

DODGE CITY AND VICINITY

Known in the 1870s and 1880s as the wickedest little city in America, this frontier town was a rendezvous for buffalo hunters, cowboys, cattlemen, railroad builders, saloonkeepers, Indians, dance-hall girls, thugs, and gamblers. Founded with the coming of the Santa Fe Railroad in 1872, Dodge City soon became a major shipping center for cattle as well as a market for buffalo hides and meat. Although the town was notorious for vice and violence, lawless elements were eventually kept in check by such "2-gun marshals" as Bat Masterson and Wyatt Earp. Today **Boot Hill,** where outlaws were once unceremoniously buried with their boots on, **Old Fort Dodge Jail,** now a museum, and a replica of **Old Front Street,** replete with saloons, serve as reminders of Dodge City's colorful past.

KENTUCKY

CUMBERLAND GAP NATIONAL HISTORICAL PARK, *southeast Kentucky, west Virginia, and north Tennessee; across via U.S. 25E*

Cumberland Gap, a natural passage through the Cumberland Mountains, was known to the Indians long before Dr. Thomas Walker discovered it in 1750. In the mid-1760s, after the French and Indian War, small hunting parties began to cross through Cumberland Gap. Daniel Boone traversed the gap as early as 1769, and after he blazed the **Wilderness Road** through the gap in 1775 settlers poured westward. Boone's Wilderness Road became the main artery of the trans-Allegheny migration that helped extend the United States' boundaries into the Northwest and westward to the Mississippi. By 1783 some 12,000 settlers had entered Kentucky, mostly through Cumberland Gap. In 1796 the Wilderness Road was widened and improved for wagon traffic. During the Civil War both Union and Confederate forces sought control of the gap, and it changed hands several times until the Federals captured it in September 1863. This national park covers almost 32 square miles. Besides the gap itself, the park includes 2 miles of the **Wilderness Road,** Civil War fortifications, and **Tri-State Peak,** where Kentucky, Tennessee, and Virginia meet.

For further information write: Box 840, Middlesboro, KY 40965

LOUISIANA

JEAN LAFITTE NATIONAL HISTORICAL PARK AND PRESERVE

This park is divided into 3 units that highlight the history and ecology of the Mississippi Delta. The **Chalmette Unit** (located southeast of New Orleans on Highway 39) was the scene of the Battle of New Orleans, Andrew Jackson's astonishing victory over superior British troops on January 8, 1815. Jackson withdrew to Chalmette Plantation in December, 1814, following a preliminary encounter that halted the advance of Sir Edward Pakenham's 7,500-man army 7 miles from New Orleans. The American defense lines at Chalmette—a fortified dry canal running from the Mississippi to an impassable swamp—proved to be the British undoing. After an unsuccessful attack on the Americans on January 1st, Pakenham launched a final strike on January 8th. Within 30 minutes Jackson's 5,000 troops decimated the British. A portion of the American defense line can still be seen in the park. Also here are the **Chalmette National Cemetery** and **Beauregard House**, an antebellum mansion that serves as the visitor center for this unit. Another visitor center in the **French Quarter Unit** is located in Jackson Square in New Orleans *(see)*. The **Barataria Unit**, located 10 miles south of New Orleans on Highway 45, focuses on the wildlife of the bayou country.

Beauregard House open: May–Oct, daily 9–6; Nov–Apr, daily 9–5

NEW ORLEANS

CABILDO NATIONAL HISTORIC LANDMARK, *709 Chartres Street*

This structure, also known as the Casa Capitular, was begun in 1795 as the seat of the Cabildo, or administrative and legislative council for Spanish Louisiana. The ceremony in which Louisiana Territory, after

The buildings of New Orleans' Vieux Carré are here framed in the intricate ironwork that is one of the hallmarks of the district.

DELTA AIR LINES

A stalwart Andrew Jackson rallies his troops against the British in this engraving of the 1815 Battle of New Orleans.

U.S. SIGNAL CORPS, NATIONAL ARCHIVES

having been under Spanish control since 1763, was receded to the French, occurred at the Cabildo on November 30, 1803. On December 20, 1803, another ceremony, representing the transfer of sovereignty of Louisiana Territory from France to the United States, took place there. The building, which was used for public offices until 1911, now contains part of the **Louisiana State Museum.**
Open: Tues–Sun 10–6

JACKSON SQUARE NATIONAL HISTORIC LANDMARK

Originally called the Place d'Armes, this square in the heart of the Vieux Carré *(see)* has been the center of the city since it was first laid out. In Jackson Square on December 20, 1803, the U.S. flag was raised for the first time over the newly purchased Louisiana Territory. Andrew Jackson was received in this square by the citizens of New Orleans after his encounter with the British at Chalmette. Jackson Square, now a tree-shaded public park, contains an equestrian statue of Jackson, a flagpole symbolizing the transfer of the Louisiana Territory to the United States, and a visitor center which is part of Jean Lafitte National Historical Park *(see)*.
Visitor Center open: May–Oct, daily 9–6; Nov–Apr, daily 9–5

OLD URSULINE CONVENT NATIONAL HISTORIC LANDMARK, *1114 Chartres Street*

Built between 1748 and 1752 on the site of a 1734 convent, this structure is one of the few remaining links to New Orleans as the French capital of Louisiana. The original convent was founded by Ursuline nuns who arrived from France in 1728. The present structure, which was extensively remodeled in 1924, is now part of the rectory of St. Mary's Italian Church.

VIEUX CARRE HISTORIC DISTRICT NATIONAL HISTORIC LANDMARK

The French Quarter, or Vieux Carré, which covers some 85 blocks, is the nucleus of the original city of New Orleans. The district, famous for its narrow streets, flower-filled courtyards, and old Creole homes with wrought-iron balconies, retains much of the flavor of early New Orleans. The city was founded in 1718 by the French governor of Louisiana, Jean Baptiste de Moyne, Sieur de Bienville, who 3 years later plotted the city into 80 rectilinear blocks. In 1722 New Orleans, named in honor of the Duc d'Orleans, Regent of France, replaced Biloxi as the capital of French Louisiana. In 1763, when France ceded Louisiana to Spain, New Orleans became the capital of Spanish Louisiana. The metropolis grew rapidly, and new buildings replaced the many structures destroyed by the fires of 1788 and 1794. After the War of 1812 New Orleans became a major port for the growing steamboat traffic on the Mississippi. Most of the structures in the Vieux Carré were built between 1794 and 1850. Many of them represent unique fusions of architectural styles, notably French, Spanish, and Greek Revival. Some of the landmarks that date back to the French and Spanish periods include the **Cabildo**, the **Ursuline Convent**, and **Jackson Square** *(see all)*. Other notable sites in the French Quarter include the **Presbytère** (NHL), reputed to be the shop operated by the pirate brothers Jean and Pierre Lafitte, and the **Bank of the United States**.

Guided tours of the French Quarter begin at the visitor center in Jackson Square.

MAINE

FORT KENT VICINITY

FORT KENT NATIONAL HISTORIC LANDMARK, ¾ mile southwest, off State 11 or 161 and U.S. 1

This fort was constructed in 1839 for the undeclared and bloodless Aroostook Border War, which concerned a boundary dispute between Maine and New Brunswick. A misunderstanding about the northeastern boundary had existed between the United States and Canada since 1783. The controversy flared up in the 1830s, when Maine lumberjacks along the Aroostook River tried to oust rival "trespassing" Canadians. Finally, in 1839, the aroused citizens of Maine and the province of New Brunswick called out their respective militias to protect their public lands. President Martin Van Buren thereupon dispatched General Winfield Scott to the area to maintain the peace and negotiate a truce with New Brunswick, which he accomplished. The dispute was finally resolved and the boundary fixed in the Webster-Ashburton Treaty of 1842. Today the original blockhouse contains a museum.

Open: Memorial Day–Labor Day, daily 9–sunset

LUBEC VICINITY

ROOSEVELT-CAMPOBELLO INTERNATIONAL PARK, *Campobello Island, New Brunswick, via F.D.R. Memorial Bridge*

Rugged Campobello Island was the summer home of Franklin D. Roosevelt from the time he was one year old in 1883 until he was stricken with polio in 1921. During his Presidency, Roosevelt returned to his "beloved island" 4 times. Today this 3,000-acre memorial to international friendship between the United States and Canada in-

cludes the 34-room Dutch colonial "cottage" where Roosevelt and his family lived after 1910; the house has been restored to its original appearance.
Open: May 26–Oct 12, daily 9–5

PROSPECT VICINITY

FORT KNOX NATIONAL HISTORIC LANDMARK, *on State 174 off U.S. 1*

The site for this granite fort was chosen during the Aroostook War *(see Fort Kent)* to defend Maine from a British invasion by way of the Penobscot River. The fort itself was begun somewhat later, in 1844, and was completed in 1864. Volunteers were garrisoned at the post during the Civil and Spanish American wars.
Open: May 1–Nov 1, daily 9–sunset

YORK

OLD YORK GAOL NATIONAL HISTORIC LANDMARK, *4 Lindsay Road, facing U.S. 1A*

The oldest English public building in the United States was begun in 1653 in accordance with the colonial laws of Massachusetts (of which Maine was a part), which stipulated that each county have a "house of correction." At that time a single stone cell—now the dungeon—with walls 2½ feet thick was constructed. Enlarged considerably in 1720, the structure served as a prison for the whole province of Maine until 1760 and was used as the York County jail until 1860. The building now contains a museum.
Open mid-June–Sept, Mon-Sat 10:30–5, Sun 1:30–5

MARYLAND

ANNAPOLIS

U.S. NAVAL ACADEMY NATIONAL HISTORIC LANDMARK, *Maryland Avenue and Hanover Street*

Since its founding in 1845 by George Bancroft, then Secretary of the Navy, the Naval Academy has produced career officers and has wielded considerable influence in naval affairs. The chapel here contains the tomb of John Paul Jones, naval hero of the Revolution. A museum displays flags, weapons, and other historical relics.
Grounds open daily 9–sunset. Museum open: Mon–Sat 9–4:45, Sun 11–4:45

ANTIETAM NATIONAL CEMETERY. *See under* SHARPSBURG

BALTIMORE

BALTIMORE & OHIO TRANSPORTATION MUSEUM AND MOUNT CLARE STATION NATIONAL HISTORIC LANDMARK, *Pratt and Poppleton streets*

Mount Clare Station initiated regular passenger train service in the United States in 1830 and in 1844 received the world's first official telegraph message, "What God hath wrought," sent by Robert Morse from Washington, D.C. **A Passenger Car Roundhouse** and an **Annex** house a historical collection of locomotives and railroad cars.
Open: Wed–Sat 10–4

FORT McHENRY NATIONAL MONUMENT AND HISTORIC SHRINE, *3 miles from Baltimore center via East Fort Avenue*

Strategically situated at the entrance to Baltimore's inner harbor, Fort McHenry bravely resisted a 25-hour bombardment by the British during the War of 1812, preventing Baltimore's occupation by the enemy and inspiring our national anthem. This star-shaped military defense, replete with bastions, batteries, magazines, and barricades, was built between 1798 and 1803 on the site of an earlier fort and was named after James McHenry of Baltimore, sometime secretary to George Washington during the Revolution and U.S. Secretary of War from 1796 to 1800. After the burning of Washington in 1814, the British planned a joint naval and land attack on Baltimore, "the great repository of the hostile spirit of the United States against England." On September 12, 1814, the British land forces encamped on the outskirts of the city. The following morning the British fleet anchored about 2 miles below Fort McHenry and began its siege. Over the next 25 hours nearly 1,800 bombs, rockets, and shells were fired by the British, but Fort McHenry suffered only moderate damage with few casualties. Francis Scott Key, a young lawyer, witnessed the event from an American truce ship on the Patapsco River. At night, when the flag was obscured, Key knew that the fort was in American hands as long as the gunfire continued. By the dawn's early light the Stars and Stripes was still flying, and Key was prompted to write "The Star-Spangled Banner." Fort McHenry functioned as an active military post, serving in every subsequent American War through World War II. Today the fort has been restored to its pre-Civil War appearance.

For further information write: Superintendent, Baltimore, MD 21230

U.S.S. *CONSTELLATION* NATIONAL HISTORIC LANDMARK, *Pier 1, Pratt Street*

Launched in 1797, this 36-gun frigate, nicknamed the Yankee Racehorse, is the nation's oldest warship. The first commissioned ship in the U.S. Navy, it saw action against the pirates in Tripoli in 1802, the British in 1812, and in the Civil War.

Open: May 16–June 15, Labor Day–Oct 15, daily 10–6; Oct 16–May 15, daily 10–4; June 16–Labor Day, daily 10–8

CHESAPEAKE & OHIO CANAL NATIONAL HISTORICAL PARK, *extending from Georgetown in Washington, D.C. to Cumberland, Maryland*

Begun on July 4, 1828, and following the Potomac River and trans-Allegheny trade route to the Ohio River, this waterway was planned to provide a much-needed transportation link between the commercial establishments of the eastern seaboard and the rich raw materials of the West. Seeing the need for developing our natural resources, Thomas Jefferson in 1806 allocated Federal funds for the construction of a national highway across the Alleghenies. The resulting National Road, completed in 1817, bore such heavy traffic that an even more economical means of transportation was sought. Water transportation, it was believed at the time, via canals and improved riverbeds would solve the problem. Ironically, the Chesapeake & Ohio Canal was begun the same day that work started on the Baltimore & Ohio Railroad at Baltimore. Among the difficulties that were encountered in the construction of this canal were shortages of building supplies, difficult negotiations to secure land for right of way, inadequate skilled labor (workers from Europe were eventually hired), disease, labor riots, and a bitter struggle with the B&O Railroad for property rights. The canal opened as the individual sections were completed. By 1850 the canal extended 184½ miles to Cumberland. Plans to continue it westward to Pittsburgh were abandoned because the B&O Railroad, finished 8 years earlier, had made the canal obsolete. An economic failure, the canal was seriously damaged in 2 floods and finally closed in 1924.

SHARPSBURG VICINITY

ANTIETAM NATIONAL BATTLEFIELD SITE, *north and east of Sharpsburg on State 34 and 65*

Also known as the Battle of Sharpsburg, the engagement that occurred at this site near the Virginia border on September 17, 1862, was the bloodiest battle of the Civil War; it also marked the turning point in the conflict between the North and South. Robert E. Lee's effort to move the war to the North was frustrated, and thenceforth the Confederate armies were placed entirely on the defensive. And the unexpected Union victory gave President Abraham Lincoln the opportunity to issue the preliminary Emancipation Proclamation 5 days later. After his victory at Manassas (the Second Battle of Bull Run) in Virginia, General Lee advanced into Maryland and moved westward, with the Federal forces under George B. McClellan, commander of the Army of the Potomac, in pursuit. Lee, with 41,000 Confederate soldiers, took up battle position at Sharpsburg near Antietam Creek. McClellan had most of his 87,000 troops in the vicinity. The fighting began at dawn on September 17 when the Union division commander Joseph Hooker launched an artillery attack on Stonewall Jackson's Confederate troops at a cornfield on the **Joseph Poffenberger Farm.** The battle raged all day over an area of 12 square miles. Scenes of heavy clashes included the **Dunkard Church, "Bloody Lane,"** which produced 4,000 casualties, and **Burnside Bridge,** where a few Confederates successfully held off Union forces. The timely arrival of another Confederate division prevented a Union rout, and the battle ended at dusk at a site now marked by the **Hawkins Zouaves Monument.** During the battle 12,410 Federal troops and 10,700 Confederates were killed or wounded. Today the battlefield is marked with 200 tablets and monuments. Vertical cannon barrels indicate where 6 generals were killed. At nearby **Antietam National Cemetery,** founded in 1865, 4,776 Federal soldiers, as well as a number of men killed in action in later wars, are buried.

For further information write: Box 158, Sharpsburg, MD 21782

MASSACHUSETTS

BOSTON

BEACON HILL HISTORIC DISTRICT NATIONAL HISTORIC LANDMARK

After the erection of the new Massachusetts State House in the 1790s, Beacon Hill became the city's most elegant residential district, home of the old "Brahmin" families. Red-brick houses—

individualized by hidden gardens, wrought-iron balconies, gas-lights, foot scrapers, and carriage houses—still delight the eye, although many have been converted into apartments. The **Harrison Gray Otis House** (a state historic landmark), at 85 Mt. Vernon Street, was designed by Charles Bulfinch and has been described as the handsomest house in Boston. **Louisburg Square** (pronounced "Lewisburg") is a private cul-de-sac maintained by the owners of the beautiful houses around the park; William Dean Howells, Louisa May Alcott, and Jenny Lind each lived on the square. **Chestnut Street** is famous for its lovely recessed doorways. Historian Francis Parkman lived at Number 50, and Edwin Booth resided at 29A; Julia Ward Howe and later John Singer Sargent lived at 13.

BOSTON COMMON

Purchased by the town of Boston from settler William Blaxton (or Blackstone) in 1634 for about $150, this historic 5-sided tract served as a training field for the military and as a grazing area for Boston's cattle. In 1638 gallows were built on one of the 4 hills on the 50-acre common; there Indians, Quakers, and other condemned individuals were executed. A ducking stool at the Frog Pond was used for "scolds and raillers," and a whipping post and stocks were built for those who profaned the Sabbath. British redcoats mustered here prior to the Battle of Bunker Hill. Various monuments and tablets on the common commemorate some of the many historic events that took place here.

BUNKER HILL NATIONAL HISTORIC LANDMARK, *Monument Square, Charlestown*

Besieged on the Boston peninsula since the battles at Lexington and Concord, the British attempted to break the siege on June 17, 1775, by storming Breed's Hill in Charlestown, which had been occupied by colonial militia under Colonel William Prescott. The ensuing battle, referred to as the Battle of Bunker Hill (which the Americans

On the single bloodiest day of the Civil War, Union troops attack at Antietam, September 17, 1862.

LIBRARY OF CONGRESS

had considered occupying but had rejected in favor of nearby Breed's Hill), ended in an American retreat; but the rebels inflicted heavy casualties on the enemy, and their valiant defense of the hill heightened the colonial determination to resist. A granite obelisk, 221 feet high, marks the site of the battle.
Open daily 9–dusk

DORCHESTER HEIGHTS NATIONAL HISTORIC SITE, *Telegraph Hill, South Boston*

In March 1776 cannon captured months earlier by Ethan Allen at Fort Ticonderoga and hauled to Boston on sleds by Henry Knox finally reached their destination, Dorchester Heights, which had been occupied by George Washington's troops. When the cannon began barraging the redcoats, General Howe, the British commander, realized that his situation was hopeless. On March 17 the British evacuated the city, giving the Americans their first major victory of the war. A white marble monument, 118 feet high, commemorates the site.

FANEUIL HILL NATIONAL HISTORIC LANDMARK, *Dock Square*

Known as the Cradle of Liberty because of the many protest meetings held here during the Revolutionary period, Faneuil Hall was built in 1742 and given to the city by Peter Faneuil, a local merchant. At street level was a public market; above was a town hall. Destroyed by fire in 1761, the structure was rebuilt, and in 1805 Charles Bulfinch enlarged it and added a third story. During the British occupation of Boston, the redcoats used the hall as a theater. Today the building, its famous grasshopper weathervane intact, houses historical paintings, a library, and a military museum.
Hall open daily 9–4

KING'S CHAPEL NATIONAL HISTORIC LANDMARK, *Tremont and School streets*

King's Chapel was erected in 1754 on the site of the first Anglican church in New England, which had been built in 1686 by the royal governor of Massachusetts. After the Revolution the chapel became America's first Unitarian church. In the adjoining burial ground are the graves of John Winthrop and other early settlers.
Open daily 10–4; closed Mon

MASSACHUSETTS STATE HOUSE NATIONAL HISTORIC LANDMARK, *Beacon Hill*

On July 4, 1795, Sam Adams and Paul Revere laid the cornerstone for a new State House: a red-brick domed structure designed by Charles Bulfinch. The Massachusetts General Court first met in the new building in January 1798. Today additions on both sides surround the original Bulfinch building. Historic documents, battle flags, and paintings depicting scenes in Massachusetts history are on display, as is the famous "sacred codfish," which hangs in the house of representatives.
Open: Mon–Fri 10–4

"OLD GRANARY" BURIAL GROUND, *Tremont Street at Bromfield Street*

So named because the town granary once stood on the site of nearby

This balloon's-eye view of Boston in 1860 is the first successful American aerial photograph.
LIBRARY OF CONGRESS

Park Street Church (where William Lloyd Garrison gave his first antislavery address in 1829), this historic burial ground contains the graves of 3 signers of the Declaration of Independence—John Hancock, Samuel Adams, and Robert Treat Paine—as well as those of Paul Revere, James Otis, and Benjamin Franklin's parents.

OLD NORTH CHURCH NATIONAL HISTORIC LANDMARK, *193 Salem Street*

Built in 1723 by William Price, a Boston print-seller and draftsman who had made a study of Christopher Wren's London churches, Old North (Christ Church Episcopal) is the oldest extant church in Boston. From its 190-foot-high steeple were hung the signal lanterns alerting colonial patriots that British troops were on their way to Lexington and Concord. In 1954 a hurricane blew the steeple down and it was replaced, but the original window from which the lanterns burned in 1775 was saved and built into the new steeple. General Thomas Gage, royal governor of the colony, is said to have watched the Battle of Bunker Hill from the steeple, and in 1817 President James Monroe received Communion here.

Open daily 9–5

OLD SOUTH MEETINGHOUSE NATIONAL HISTORIC LANDMARK, *Washington and Milk streets*

Like Faneuil Hall, Old South was the scene of angry public protests during the Revolutionary period. James Otis, Sam Adams, and John Hancock all spoke from the pulpit, and it was here that the signal to begin the Boston Tea Party was given. During the war General Burgoyne removed the pews and pulpit and established a riding school for his troops in the meetinghouse. Directly across the street, at 17 Milk Street, is the site of **Benjamin Franklin's Birthplace.**

Open: Apr–Oct, daily 9:30–4:45; Nov–Mar, Mon–Fri 10–3:45, Sat 10–4:45

OLD STATE HOUSE NATIONAL HISTORIC LANDMARK, *Washington Street at State*

It was in front of the Old State House, built in 1713 as headquarters for the royal governors, that the famous Boston Massacre took place in March 1770. Six years later the Declaration of Independence was read to excited Bostonians from the east balcony. In 1789 George Washington viewed a parade in his honor from another balcony.

Open: Mon–Fri 10–4, Sat 9:30–5, Sun 11–5

PAUL REVERE HOUSE NATIONAL HISTORIC LANDMARK, *19-21 North Square*

The oldest frame house in Boston, built around 1670, was purchased in 1770 by Paul Revere. From here on April 18, 1775, the silversmith began his famous "midnight ride." The house has been restored and furnished in the style of the period when the patriot lived here (1770–1800).

Open: Apr 15–Oct, daily 9:30–5:30; Nov–Apr 14, Tues–Sun 10–4

U.S.S. *CONSTITUTION* NATIONAL HISTORIC LANDMARK, *Boston Naval Shipyard, Charlestown*

Launched in 1797, the *Constitution* won fame during the War of 1812 when she was victorious in several battles against British vessels. The 44-gun frigate, called Old Ironsides because of the copper-sheath-

ing made for her by Paul Revere, was due to be dismantled in 1830, but Oliver Wendell Holmes's poem "Old Ironsides" aroused a public outcry.
Open daily 9:30–4

CONCORD AND VICINITY

ANTIQUARIAN MUSEUM, *½ mile southeast on State 2A*

This brick building contains 15 period rooms, furnished authentically with antiques dating as far back as 1685. Other attractions include a replica of Ralph Waldo Emerson's study with the original furnishings; the lantern that hung on the Old North Church on the night of Paul Revere's ride, a diorama of the Concord battle, and a room displaying Thoreau's books, flute, and some of the equipment he used at Walden.
Open summer: daily 10-4:30; rest of the year: daily 10–3:30

EMERSON HOUSE NATIONAL HISTORIC LANDMARK, *Cambridge Turnpike and State 2A*

Ralph Waldo Emerson built this square white house in 1820 and lived in it from 1835 until he died in 1882. When the philosopher traveled to Europe, his friend Thoreau occupied the dwelling. The Victorian interior has been preserved, with Emerson's furniture and possessions on view.
Open mid–Apr-Oct, Thurs, Fri, Sat 1–4:30

MINUTEMAN NATIONAL HISTORICAL PARK

After the bloody encounter at Lexington *(see)* on April 19, 1775, the British troops marched on to Concord and began to search for and destroy the rebels' military supplies. Massed on a hillside above the **Old North Bridge**, some 400 militia and minutemen saw smoke rising from the center of town and assumed erroneously that the British were burning Concord. Advancing under orders not to shoot unless fired upon, the Americans encountered at the bridge 3 British companies, which volleyed, killing 2 minutemen. In the ensuing fight Americans killed 2 redcoats, fatally wounded another, and hit 9 more; the astonished British retreated, regrouped with their other units, and then began marching back to Lexington. At **Meriam's Corner**, however, Americans began firing on them from behind stone walls, trees, and fences; their numbers swelled by newcomers who had heard of the encounters at Lexington and the Old North Bridge, the local patriots cut across fields and maintained a steady harassment of the retreating troops. By firing upon the king's soldiers on that momentous day, Americans marked the end of a long political battle and the beginning of the shooting war that was to lead to independence. Minuteman National Historical Park is composed of 750 acres in 3 units. **Battle Road Unit**, between Meriam's Corner in Concord and Fiske Hill in Lexington, preserves 4 miles of historic battle route. The Battle Road visitor center off Route 2A in Lexington is located in the unit, where a film, "To Keep Our Liberty," a sound and light program, and exhibits are available. In the **North Bridge Unit** stands Daniel Chester French's Minuteman Statue, and a visitor center on Liberty Street has other exhibits. **The Wayside Unit** features the home of Samuel Whitney, who was Concord's muster master in 1775; Nathaniel Hawthorne, the Alcotts, and Margaret Sidney lived there in later years. Throughout the park, modern buildings are being removed and the historic houses and landscape are being restored to their

Lexington prepares for the centennial celebration of the start of the American Revolution.

CONCORD FREE PUBLIC LIBRARY

1775 appearance.
North Bridge Visitor Center open daily 8:30–5; Battle Road Visitor Center open: Apr–Nov, daily 8:30–5; Wayside Visitor Center open: Apr–Nov, daily 9:15–9:45; Dec–Mar, closed Mon

OLD MANSE NATIONAL HISTORIC LANDMARK, *Monument Street*
Built in 1769 on the banks of the Concord River, this clapboard, gambrel-roofed house was the home of the Reverend William Emerson, who stood in his yard on April 19, 1775, and watched the minutemen fight the redcoats at the Old North Bridge. His grandson, philosopher Ralph Waldo Emerson, spent much of his boyhood in the house, and Nathaniel Hawthorne was a tenant there from 1842 to 1846.
Open: June 1–Oct 15, Mon–Sat 10–4:30, Sun 1–4:30; Apr 19–Memorial Day, Oct 16–Nov 1 by appointment

ORCHARD HOUSE NATIONAL HISTORIC LANDMARK, *399 Lexington Road*
Louisa May Alcott wrote the first part of *Little Women* in this house, which she called Apple Stump because it stood in an orchard. Actually 2 old houses were joined together and refurbished by the Alcott family; the 2½-story dwelling was the writer's home from 1858 to 1877.
Open: Apr–Sept 15, Mon–Sat 10–4:30, Sun 1–4:30; Sept 16–Oct, daily 1–4:30; Nov–Mar by appointment

WALDEN POND NATIONAL HISTORIC LANDMARK, *1½ miles south on State 126*

A cairn and tablet on the north shore of this 64-acre pond mark the site of Henry David Thoreau's famous cabin, erected in 1845. The naturalist-poet remained there for more than 2 years, "living deep and sucking out all the marrow of life." His book *Walden* is an account of his experience. The area is now a state reservation, where vacationers can camp, swim, and fish.

WRIGHT TAVERN NATIONAL HISTORIC LANDMARK, *2 Lexington Road*

Built in 1747, this tavern was a gathering place for minutemen on April 19, 1775, and a resting place for the British officers who later that day sent their men to Concord. Now a gift shop.
Open daily

DEERFIELD

OLD DEERFIELD VILLAGE NATIONAL HISTORIC LANDMARK, *Route 5*

First settled in 1669, Deerfield was the northwest frontier of New England and the target of French and Indian attacks. In 1675, during King Philip's War, the Bloody Brook Massacre resulted in the evacuation of the town, which was deserted for 7 years. The great Deerfield Massacre of 1704, during Queen Anne's War, saw half the town burned, 49 residents killed, and 111 others taken to Canada as prisoners. Among the many historic houses open to visitors today are the **Frary House**, parts of which were built before the 1704 massacre but which was rebuilt during the mid-18th century as a tavern (Benedict Arnold is believed to have stopped there); the **John Sheldon Indian House**, a reproduction of the house that was the focal point of the 1704 massacre —its original door, split by a tomahawk, is on view in **Memorial Hall**, a museum of Indian and early American artifacts; the **Hall Tavern** and 18th-century inn moved here from its original site at Charlemont on the Mohawk Trail; the **Asa Stebbins House**, built in the 1790s for the son of the country's richest landowner; and the **Wilson Printing House**, an 1816 printing shop with a working hand press.

HANCOCK

HANCOCK SHAKER VILLAGE NATIONAL HISTORIC LANDMARK, *U.S. 20*

Exemplifying Mother Anne Lee's injunction to "put your hands to work and your hearts to God," this restored community of 1790 is marked by functional simplicity. There are 18 buildings, including a unique round stone barn, and some 65 rooms furnished with authentic Shaker items.
Open: June-Oct 15, daily 9:30–5

HARVARD

FRUITLANDS MUSEUMS NATIONAL HISTORIC LANDMARK, *Prospect Hill Road*

Fruitlands is the 18th-century farmhouse in which Bronson Alcott, father of Louisa May Alcott, lived from June 1843 to January 1844 while attempting to establish a transcendental community. On the

same grounds are an **American Indian Museum**, the **Old Shaker House**, and a gallery featuring artists of the Hudson River school.
Open: Memorial Day-Sept 30, Tues-Sun 1–5

LEXINGTON

BUCKMAN TAVERN NATIONAL HISTORIC LANDMARK, *Bedford Street*

Built in 1703, this tavern was the rallying place of the minutemen on the morning of April 19, 1775. Warned by Paul Revere and others that a British force was approaching, local rebels gathered here to await the redcoats' arrival.
Open: Apr 19-Oct 31, Mon-Sat 10–4, Sun 1–5; August until 8 p.m.

HANCOCK-CLARKE HOUSE NATIONAL HISTORIC LANDMARK, *35 Hancock Street*

Samuel Adams and John Hancock, Revolutionary leaders, were guests in this 1698 parsonage on the night of April 18, 1775, when Paul Revere warned them of the British approach.
Open: Apr 19-Oct 31, Mon-Sat 10–4, Sun 1–5

LEXINGTON GREEN NATIONAL HISTORIC LANDMARK

Under orders to confiscate military supplies stored by the rebels at Concord, Lieutenant Colonel Francis Smith and 700 British regulars arrived at Lexington Green at dawn on April 19, 1775. They were met there by 50 or 60 minutemen, who had been told by Captain John Parker, "Stand your ground, don't fire unless fired upon, but if they mean to have a war, let it begin here." No one knows who fired the first shot, but it was followed by a British barrage and bayonet attack. Eight Americans were killed and 10 wounded. The cheering British regrouped and marched on to Concord.

MINUTEMAN NATIONAL HISTORICAL PARK. *See under* CONCORD

MONROE TAVERN, *1332 Massachusetts Avenue*

Built in 1695 and subsequently altered, this building was used as headquarters by British troops on April 19, 1775. In 1789 George Washington was entertained at a dinner here.
Open: Apr 19-Oct 31, Mon-Sat 10–4, Sun 1–5

NANTUCKET HISTORIC DISTRICT NATIONAL HISTORIC LANDMARK

Settled by men and women fleeing the religious intolerance of mainland communities, Nantucket developed into one of the world's great whaling ports. By 1768, 125 whaling ships were based here. Among the buildings open to visitors are the **Jethro Coffin House** (NHL), which was built in 1686 and is the oldest house on the island; the **1800 House**, a typical Nantucket dwelling of that period; and the **Hadwen House-Satler Memorial**, an elegant mansion built for a wealthy whale-oil merchant. The **Whaling Museum** has one of the nation's outstanding exhibits on that bygone activity, and the **Maria Mitchell Memorial House** preserves the birthplace of America's first woman astronomer. Other sites of interest are the **Old Gaol**, **Old Mill**, and **Quaker Meeting House**.

NEW BEDFORD DISTRICT NATIONAL HISTORIC LANDMARK

From 1820 until the Civil War, New Bedford was the country's greatest whaling port; in 1845 alone, some 158,000 barrels of sperm oil, 272,000 barrels of whale oil, and 3 million pounds of whalebone were brought in by the 10,000 seamen who sailed on New Bedford ships. In recent years historic buildings in the now-decayed waterfront area have been restored. Among the leading sites are the **Seamen's Bethel**, the historic church that Herman Melville used as a setting in *Moby Dick*; the **Third District Court**, an Italianate Revival structure built in 1853; the **Whaling Museum** containing superb exhibits including a half-size model of the whaling bark *Lagoda* with all her equipment; the **Rotch Counting House**, and the **U.S. Customhouse** (NHL).

PLYMOUTH AND VICINITY

COLE'S HILL NATIONAL HISTORIC LANDMARK, *Carver Street*

Of the 102 persons who landed at Plymouth Rock in December 1620, more than half died during that first winter. Many were buried on Cole's Hill, a site now marked by a statue of the Indian chief Massasoit.

MAYFLOWER II, State Pier, Water Street

This is a full-size replica of the ship that brought the Pilgrims to America. The original vessel carried 102 passengers and 25 crewmen to the New World on a voyage that took 66 days.
Open: Apr-Nov, daily 9–5

PLYMOUTH PLANTATION, *2 miles south off State 3A*

This is a full-scale replica of the Pilgrim colony as it appeared in 1627. The fort-meetinghouse overlooks houses and gardens, workshops, and an Indian campsite. There are demonstrations of 17th-century crafts by costumed guides.
Open: Apr-Nov, daily 9–5

PLYMOUTH ROCK, *Water Street*

A granite portico now shelters the rock that according to tradition was the Pilgrims' steppingstone to the New World. The date 1620 has been carved on the rock.

QUINCY

ADAMS NATIONAL HISTORIC SITE, *135 Adams Street*

Four generations of one of America's most distinguished families lived in this Georgian clapboard house, which John Adams called Peacefield but which subsequent generations referred to as the Old House. The oldest section was built in 1731 by Major Leonard Vassall, a West Indian sugar planter. John Adams was minister to Great Britain when he bought the house in 1787; the next year he added several new rooms and moved in. Adams and his wife retired to Peacefield when his Presidency ended in 1801 and lived there until his death in 1826. His son, President John Quincy Adams, made the Old House his summer home, as did his son, diplomat-historian Charles Francis Adams, who erected the stone library adjoining the garden. His sons, Brooks and Henry Adams, spent many summers here. It was occupied until Brooks' death in 1927 and is shown with the furnishings collected by the family in the 140 years they lived here. The historic site also includes the **United Parish Church** (NHL) built by the Adams family and the birthplaces of the two presidents *(see).*
Open: Apr 19-Nov 10, daily 9–5

JOHN ADAMS BIRTHPLACE NATIONAL HISTORIC LANDMARK, *133 Franklin Street*

John Adams, second President of the United States, was born here in 1735. The saltbox house was erected in 1681.

Open: Apr 19-Oct 15, daily 9–5

JOHN QUINCY ADAMS BIRTHPLACE NATIONAL HISTORIC LANDMARK, *141 Franklin Street*

After his marriage to Abigail Smith in 1764, John Adams moved into this house, which had been left to him by his father; Adams used the kitchen as his law office. John Quincy Adams, the sixth President, was born here in 1767.

Open: Apr 19-Oct 15, daily 9–5

SALEM

CHESTNUT STREET AREA STATE HISTORIC LANDMARK

Laid out in 1796 and enlarged in 1804, Chestnut Street is a monument to Salem's prosperity in the 18th century, when ships owned by local men traded all over the world. The affluent shipowners, merchants, and other distinguished townsmen built elegant mansions, many of them designed by the brilliant architect Samuel McIntire. Most of the homes were completed about 1830 and are superb examples of the Federal style. **Hamilton Hall** (NHL), a McIntire building on the corner of Chestnut and Cambridge, is regarded as a link between the simple houses of the turn of the century and the more ornate homes built in the following decades.

ESSEX INSTITUTE, *132 Essex Street*

In addition to a large museum containing art and historical objects from the colonial and Federal periods, the institute maintains several excellent examples of Salem homes from different periods; all have been restored and furnished authentically. The **John Ward House** (NHL), dating from 1684, is the oldest. The **Crowninshield-Bentley House** was built in 1727, and the **Peirce-Nichols House** (NHL) was erected in 1782. Samuel McIntire designed it and also the magnificent **Gardner-Pingree House** (NHL), built in 1804 for a sea captain and considered McIntire's finest work. McIntire also remodeled the **Assembly House** (which had been built in 1782 as an assembly hall) as a home. The **Andrew-Safford House**, built in 1818, is now the residence of the Institute's director.

HOUSE OF SEVEN GABLES STATE HISTORIC LANDMARK, *54 Turner Street*

Built about 1668 by Captain John Turner, this house was visited several times by Nathaniel Hawthorne, who made it famous when he used its name for his novel. Six other buildings are now preserved as part of the House of Seven Gables complex. Among them are **Hawthorne's Birthplace**, a simple gambrel-roofed house built about 1750 and moved here later, and the **Retire Beckett House**, built in 1655 by the founder of a shipbuilding family.

Open: July 1-Labor Day, daily 9:30–6:30; Labor Day-June 30, daily 10–4:30

SALEM MARITIME NATIONAL HISTORIC SITE, *Derby Street*

Founded in 1626, Salem was the first town in the Massachusetts Bay Colony. Fishing and shipping were the primary industries, and by 1643 fish, lumber, and provisions were being sent to the West Indies, where they were exchanged for sugar and molasses; those items were brought home and made into rum. Later Portugal and Spain became prime markets for dried fish. Restrictive measures passed by the English Parliament after 1763 brought this thriving trade to a standstill, and during the Revolution the captains of Salem aided the colonial cause by becoming privateers and preying on English ships. In the prosperous years after the war, Salem ships voyaged all over the world, and after the discovery of gold in California, local shipowners reaped large profits by sailing around Cape Horn to San Francisco. However, Salem's harbor was too shallow to accommodate the larger ships of the latter half of the 19th century, and Boston and New York replaced her as leading seaports. Visitors to the National Historic Site may see **Derby Wharf**, which extends 2,000 feet into the harbor and was one of the great mercantile centers of the young United States; the **Custom House**, directly opposite the wharf, which was built in 1819 (Nathaniel Hawthorne worked there as surveyor of the port of Salem from 1846 to 1849); **Derby House**, erected by merchant Elias Haskett Derby in 1761–62; the **West India Goods Store**; the **Scale House**, where various weighing devices were kept; and the **Bonded Warehouse**, where cargoes were stored.

Open daily 8:30–5

THE WITCH HOUSE, *310½ Essex Street*

Built in 1642, this was the home of Jonathan Corwin, one of the judges who presided during the witchcraft trials that resulted in 20 executions in 1692. Some preliminary witchcraft examinations took place in the house, although the actual trials were conducted in the **Courthouse**, at Washington and Federal streets.

Open: Mar 1–Labor Day, daily 10–6; Sept-Nov, daily 10–5

SOUTH SUDBURY

WAYSIDE INN STATE HISTORIC LANDMARK, *Wayside Inn Road*

Built by Samuel Howe sometime between 1686 and 1702, this is believed to be the oldest operating inn in the United States. Known first as Howe Tavern and later as the Red Horse, the inn was visited by Henry Wadsworth Longfellow, who immortalized it in 1862 in "Tales of a Wayside Inn." Henry Ford acquired the inn in 1923.

Open daily

STURBRIDGE

OLD STURBRIDGE VILLAGE, *junction of Massachusetts Turnpike, I-86, U.S. 20, and State 131*

Eighteenth-century New England comes back to life in Old Sturbridge, an authentic re-creation of an old farming community. More than 40 buildings are open to visitors. Clustered around the village green are the meetinghouse, general store, and various shops and private homes. Elsewhere on the grounds are a working farm, a gristmill, a sawmill, and numerous buildings where men and women in authentic costumes demonstrate various crafts and skills just as they were performed a century ago.

Open: Apr-Oct, daily 9–5; Nov-Mar, Tues-Sun 10–4

DEARBORN

GREENFIELD VILLAGE, *Village Road and Oakwood Boulevard*

The physical layout of this community is that of a typical American village of the 19th century, but the idea behind it is completely novel. In effect, this is a collective historical site with more than 200 structures representing famous homes or places of work; some are reconstructions, but many are authentic buildings moved from their original locations. Included are the homes of Noah Webster, Luther Burbank, Stephen Foster, and Henry Ford; the courthouse where Lincoln practiced law; the Dayton cycle shop of the Wright brothers; and the Menlo Park laboratory of Thomas Edison. There is also a Mississippi River paddle-wheel steamboat, which floats on a pond. *Open daily 9–5, Sun 9–6*

HENRY FORD MUSEUM, *Village Road and Oakwood Boulevard*

Built by Ford and dedicated to Edison, this 14-acre museum has replicas of Independence Hall, Congress Hall, and the old city hall of Philadelphia. Exhibits trace the development of American industry, agriculture, transportation, communications, science, education, home

When it was completed in 1887, Mackinac Island's Grand Hotel boasted that its 627-foot verandah was the "longest hotel porch in the world."

WAYNE ANDREWS

furnishings, and interior design. There is a separate exhibit of Ford's personal belongings, together with a street of early American shops that display and demonstrate preindustrial crafts of the gunsmith, locksmith, and others.
Open daily 9–5

MACKINAW CITY AND VICINITY

FORT MICHILIMACKINAC NATIONAL HISTORIC LANDMARK, *near Mackinac Bridge at the terminus of U.S. 31*

This was the predecessor of Fort Mackinac *(see Mackinac Island)*, but its history dates from 1715, when the French built an outpost in an area marked by busy trade with the Indians. The fort passed into British hands in 1761, when the conclusion of the French and Indian War marked the end of France's North American empire. For some 20 years Fort Michilimackinac was the most important British outpost on the Great Lakes, though in 1763 the garrison suffered heavily during Pontiac's Indian uprising. Between 1779 and 1781, fearing that this mainland fort could not be defended against American raids, the British abandoned it and erected a new fort on Mackinac Island. The site of old Fort Michilimackinac was determined by archaeological investigation; today the fort has been completely restored as a fortified town.

MACKINAC ISLAND NATIONAL HISTORIC LANDMARK, *across the Straits of Mackinac*

Historic **Fort Mackinac** is the principal attraction here, though by no means the only one. One of the oldest existing forts in the United States, it was begun by the British in 1780 and remained in active service until 1895. It first came into American hands in 1796. The British again gained possession during the War of 1812, but after 1815 the outpost was under American control again. The stone ramparts, the three blockhouses, the officers' quarters, and the sally ports are all from the original fort; the other structures that are part of the overall design date from the late 1820s to the late 1870s. Nearby **Fort Holmes** is a reconstructed log building erected by the British during the War of 1812. There are also many points of interest connected with the thriving fur trade of the period from 1815 to about 1840, and with early community life following the cessation of hostilities. Among these are **Astor House**, which served as the headquarters of the American Fur Company; **Robert Stuart House**, agency house of the company; **Beaumont Memorial**, a reconstruction of the company store; **Biddle House**, which probably was built before 1800 and is believed to be the oldest surviving residential structure on the island; **Mathew Geary House**; the **Indian Dormitory**, built in 1838 to house visiting Indians who had business with the Indian Agency on the island; and **Mission House** and **Mission Church**.

MINNESOTA

MINNEAPOLIS AND VICINITY

FORT SNELLING NATIONAL HISTORIC LANDMARK, *confluence of the Mississippi and Minnesota rivers off State 5 and 55*

Established in 1819 on land obtained from the Sioux Indians in 1805 by Captain Zebulon Pike, this post was the northwestern link in a

chain of forts extending from Lake Michigan to the Missouri River. For the next 30 years, garrisons at Fort Snelling oversaw affairs with the Sioux and Chippewa Indians, controlled traffic on both rivers, operated a local fur-trade depot, and acted as the only police and government for an area of 90,000 square miles. After the Minnesota Territory was created in 1848 and the capital situated at St. Paul, the post's frontier duty was over. Fort Snelling was reactivated during the Sioux uprising of 1862, and it played a supporting role when the site of conflict between Indians and settlers shifted west. From the Civil War until World War II, Fort Snelling served as a training center for troops. Of the original structures, the **Round Tower** is believed to be the oldest building in Minnesota.
Open: June-Labor Day, daily 10–5; May, Sept, Oct, Mon-Fri 9–4:30, Sat, Sun 10–5; visitor center open daily 9–4:30

MISSISSIPPI

NATCHEZ AND VICINITY

CONNELLY'S TAVERN ON ELLICOTT'S HILL NATIONAL HISTORIC LANDMARK, *Jefferson and Canal streets*

In defiance of the Spanish, who had governed Natchez since 1779, the Stars and Stripes was first raised at this tavern in 1797. The following year Mississippi became a U.S. territory.
Open daily 9–5

LONGWOOD (NUTT'S FOLLY) NATIONAL HISTORIC LANDMARK, *1½ miles southeast*

Designed in 1860 by the architect Samuel Sloan for Dr. Haller Nutt, this 5-story mansion, with its glass-enclosed "Moorish" tower, was the largest and most ornate octagon house in the nation. The outbreak of the Civil War prevented the structure's completion.
Open daily 9–5, except during Pilgrimage in Mar and Oct

VICKSBURG

VICKSBURG *NATIONAL MILITARY PARK, adjoining Vicksburg*

This park was the scene of the siege of Vicksburg in 1863, the decisive Civil War campaign in the West that gave the Union control of the Mississippi River and divided the Confederacy in two. Strategically situated on high bluffs overlooking the Mississippi, Vicksburg, with its almost impregnable defenses, was known as the Gibraltar of the Confederacy and was the key link in a chain of Confederate fortifications extending from Louisville, Kentucky, to New Orleans, Louisiana. Its capture was considered essential to the Union. After Federal attempts to seize Vicksburg by land and amphibious assault failed in 1862, General Ulysses S. Grant, on May 18, 1863, launched a campaign to take the stronghold by siege. After 47 days the beleaguered city, defended by Confederates under General John C. Pemberton, surrendered on July 4. Today the remains of 9 major Confederate forts, 13 Union approaches, miles of breastworks, gun emplacements, and rifle pits, as well as 1,600 monuments marking the positions of the armies, are preserved. About 2 miles north of town is the **Vicksburg National Cemetery**, where 17,912 soldiers are buried.
For further information write: Box 349, Vicksburg, MS 39180

Longwood, Dr. Haller Nutt's exotic villa near Natchez, was never finished because its Philadelphia building crew fled north in 1861.
MISSISSIPPI DEPARTMENT OF ARCHIVES AND HISTORY

MISSOURI

HANNIBAL

MARK TWAIN BOYHOOD HOME NATIONAL HISTORIC LANDMARK, *208 Hill Street*

Samuel Clemens spent his boyhood in this house from the time he was 4 in 1839 until 1853. Using the pen name Mark Twain, he later wrote *Huckleberry Finn* and *The Adventures of Tom Sawyer*, both of which reflect his boyhood experiences here.

Open: June-Aug, daily 8–6; Sept-Dec, Mar, daily 9–5; Jan, Feb, daily 10–4

INDEPENDENCE

HARRY S TRUMAN NATIONAL HISTORIC SITE, *North Delaware Street*

This Victorian house was the home of President Harry S Truman from the time he left Washington in 1953 until his death in 1972. It is shown as it was during his lifetime. The house is located within the **Harry S Truman Historic District** (NHL) which also includes the **Truman Memorial Library and Museum** and the President's grave site.

Open: Apr-Dec, daily 9–4:45; Jan-Mar, closed Mon

ST. LOUIS

EADS BRIDGE NATIONAL HISTORIC LANDMARK, *spanning the Mississippi at Washington Street*

Designed by James B. Eads and completed in 1874, this cantilevered arch bridge of iron and steel contained structural innovations that established a precedent for bridge building throughout the world. Carrying a railroad on its lower deck and a road at its upper level, the bridge was an important factor in the development of St. Louis and the trans-Mississippi West.

JEFFERSON NATIONAL EXPANSION MEMORIAL NATIONAL HISTORIC SITE, *between Washington and Poplar streets*

Situated on the site of the original village of St. Louis, which was founded by Pierre Laclède in 1764, this memorial commemorates the vast expansion of the United States following Thomas Jefferson's Louisiana Purchase of 1803. This historic acquisition doubled the area of the young republic, and assured this nation a major role in the settlement of North America. Soaring 630 feet high, a catenary arch of stainless steel, designed by Eero Saarinen, is symbolic of St. Louis' gateway location; the city was the hub of mid-continental commerce, transportation, and culture, and the meeting place for pioneers starting west. Within this park stand the **Old Courthouse**, where Dred Scott made his legal appeal for freedom and focused national attention on the slavery issue, and the **Old Cathedral**, completed in 1834 on land designated earlier by Pierre Laclède for religious purposes. The **Gateway Arch** houses the Museum of Westward Expansion.

For further information write: 11 N. 4th St., St. Louis, MO 63102

MONTANA

CUSTER BATTLEFIELD NATIONAL MONUMENT, *15 miles south of Hardin on the Crow reservation*

On June 25–26, 1876, one of the most famous battles in American history took place on this site, the scene of Custer's last stand. It was precipitated by a Federal government order that the Indians of the northern plains return to their reservations by January 31 of that year. The Sioux and Cheyenne, who had left their reservations because they did not recognize an earlier peace agreement as valid and because some regarded the boundaries of the reservation as limiting their movements, decided to defy the ultimatum and rallied around Sitting Bull, Crazy Horse, and other famous chiefs. U.S. troops, called upon to enforce the order, included the Seventh Cavalry regiment under Lieutenant Colonel George A. Custer. In an engagement that has become legendary, Custer and some 225 soldiers in his immediate command, severely outnumbered, were surrounded in the **Valley of the Little Big Horn** and destroyed to a man. Seven remaining companies of the regiment suffered heavy casualties before the approach of reinforcements caused the Indians to withdraw. The national monument includes both the ridge where Custer and his men were annihilated and the Reno-Benteen defense site where the other major action took place. A cluster of markers indicates the location where the last members of Custer's battalion are thought to have fallen. A visitor center contains maps, photographs, and exhibits that re-create the action. A national cemetery in the immediate area also houses the remains of soldiers killed in

This rousing 1881 lithograph is one of dozens that recalled the last ghastly moments of Custer's command.

LIBRARY OF CONGRESS

other Indian engagements. Visitors are attracted as well by the annual Crow Indian fair and rodeo, accompanied by dances and ceremonies.

For further information write: Superintendent, Crow Agency, MT 59022

NEBRASKA

GERING VICINITY

SCOTTS BLUFF NATIONAL MONUMENT, *3 miles west on State 92*

Scotts Bluff, which rises 800 feet above the surrounding North Platte valley floor and 4,649 feet above sea level, was named for a pioneer fur trapper who died in the vicinity about 1828. The monument on this site, overlooking the **Oregon Trail**, marks successive periods in the settlement of the West. After the fur traders came the migrants who from 1843 traveled along the Oregon Trail. Brigham Young and his company of Mormons followed not long after, and the discovery of gold in California in 1848 brought new waves of pioneers. Remains of the famous trail, worn by wagon wheels, are still visible. A visitor center tells the story of this westward movement, and the **Oregon Trail Museum**, at the base of the bluff, contains paintings by William Henry Jackson. In the decade beginning in 1860, nearby **Mitchell Pass** was used by riders of the pony express and by builders of the first transcontinental telegraph.

For further information write: Box 427, Gering, NE 69341

NEVADA

VIRGINIA CITY AND VICINITY

COMSTOCK LODE, *outside of town*

Discovered in 1859, the 2½-mile-long Comstock Lode—named after the prospector Henry Comstock, who staked part of the original claim—was one of the world's richest deposits of lode silver and gold and produced more than $300 million in high-grade ore. Wealth from the lode helped to build Virginia City and San Francisco, to finance the Civil War, and to make Nevada a state by 1864. Today the sites of some of the major mines are marked by large yellow dumps.

VIRGINIA CITY HISTORIC DISTRICT NATIONAL HISTORIC LANDMARK

Founded in 1859, the year of the discovery of the Comstock Lode *(see)*, Virginia City flourished for 20 years as the most prosperous mining metropolis in Nevada and the prototype for similar boom towns throughout the West. During the Civil War Comstock silver, shipped east from Virginia City's Wells Fargo office, helped finance the Union cause. Nevada's first newspaper, the *Territorial Enterprise* (founded at Genoa in 1857), on which Samuel Clemens and Bret Harte worked as reporters, was published at Virginia City. By 1876 it boasted a population of 30,000, 4 banks, 6 churches, 100 saloons, and the only elevator between Chicago and San Francisco. In 1873 the Consolidated Virginia Mine, the largest Comstock discovery of all, opened; it eventually yielded $234 million of ore. In 1875 a fire destroyed most of Virginia City, which was subsequently rebuilt. By 1880 the richest mines in the area were exhausted, and

Virginia City began to decline. Today Nevada's largest ghost town has been restored to its 1870 appearance. Such structures as **Piper's Opera House** and **The Castle**, a Victorian mansion built in 1868 by Robert Graves, a millionaire mine superintendent, attest to Virginia City's former prosperity.
Opera House open: Memorial Day-Sept, daily 11–5; The Castle open: May-Oct, daily 11–5

NEW HAMPSHIRE

MT. WASHINGTON COG RAILWAY, *Base Station Road, 6 miles off U.S. 302 from Fabyan-Bretton Woods*
The second steepest cog railway in the world, and the first of its kind, was conceived by Herrick and Walter Aiken and Walter Marsh; it was completed in 1869 at a cost of $139,500. Made safe by a toothed wheel and ratchet, this railway makes the 3-mile trip to the 6,293-foot summit at a grade of 1 foot in 4.
Trips: Memorial Day–Mid-Oct, daily 8–5 weather permitting

PORTSMOUTH AND VICINITY, *southeast New Hampshire*
Originally known as Strawberry Banke because of the wild strawberries found growing along the riverbanks, Portsmouth (as it was renamed in 1653) was founded in 1630 and was the first permanent settlement on the Piscataqua River. Situated on an excellent harbor and possessing abundant timber resources, Portsmouth soon became a flourishing seaport town, where shipbuilding and other mercantile interests thrived during the 18th and 19th centuries. Preserved today along Portsmouth's winding streets are many reminders of its former prosperity. In the Old South End more than 30 early American buildings are being reconstructed as part of the **Strawberry Banke Restoration Project**. Representing a variety of architectural styles, the city's famous houses include the **Richard Jackson House** (NHL), erected in 1664 and the oldest extant frame dwelling in New Hampshire; the **Macpheadris-Warner House** (NHL), built between 1718 and 1723 in the early-Georgian style popular in New England colonies; the high-Georgian **Wentworth-Gardner House** (NHL), built by ship's carpenters in 1760; and the late-Georgian **Moffat-Ladd House** (NHL), raised about 1764, which later was the home of William Whipple, a signer of the Declaration of Independence. Also in Portsmouth are the **John Paul Jones House** (NHL), where the Revolutionary naval hero lodged while his ships, the *America* and *Ranger*, were being fitted; and the **Governor John Langdon Mansion Memorial** (NHL), which was built in 1784 by the first pro tempore president of the U.S. Senate, a signer of the Constitution, and the man who informed George Washington of his election as President. About 2 miles south of town at Little Harbor is the rambling **Wentworth-Coolidge Mansion** (NHL), which, begun in 1695 and enlarged in 1730 and 1750, was the home and headquarters of Benning Wentworth, whom King George appointed the first royal governor of the province of New Hampshire in 1741.
Strawberry Banke open: May-Oct, daily 10–5

CAPE MAY HISTORIC DISTRICT NATIONAL HISTORIC LANDMARK

One of the oldest Atlantic coast resorts, Cape May in the 19th century attracted America's most prominent political and social figures. Presidents Lincoln, Grant, Pierce, Buchanan, and Harrison vacationed here, as did Horace Greeley, John Wanamaker, and wealthy society leaders. In the summer of 1847 a mob of admirers chased Henry Clay up and down the beach and when they caught him snipped pieces of his hair for souvenirs. In 1903 the first Ford agency got its first car from Henry Ford, who lost a beach race and had to sell the car to pay for his train fare back to Detroit. Many of the 19th-century structures, including the verandaed hotels that face the ocean, still stand.

WASHINGTON CROSSING VICINITY

McKONKEY FERRY MUSEUM, *Washington Crossing State Park*

This restored colonial building represents the tavern where Washington rested briefly after his famous crossing of the Delaware River in 1776. After the American Army's crushing defeat in New York and its retreat across New Jersey and the Delaware River late in 1776, General Howe decided to end the British campaign for the winter rather than pursue Washington's tattered forces. Howe established a chain of British posts in New Jersey and sat back to wait for spring. Washington, however, decided on a desperate, daring offensive: needing an American victory to bolster troop morale and encourage reenlistment, he decided to cross the flooded, ice-jammed, nearly impassable Delaware and surprise the British garrison at Trenton. On the night of December 25, in a gale-driven sleet, his main division of 2,400 men—shivering, thinly dressed, many of them shoeless—began to cross at McKonkey Ferry, 9 miles above Trenton. (**The Washington Crossing Site** is a National Historic Landmark.) Colonel John Glover's regiment of sailors and fishermen from Marblehead maneuvered every available boat back and forth across the swollen river, constantly fending off huge ice slabs. Not until 4 in the morning of December 26 was the crossing completed. Washington ended a short rest at the McKonkey Ferry House, and the march to Trenton and an important American victory began.

Open by appointment

WEST ORANGE

EDISON NATIONAL HISTORIC SITE, *Main Street and Lakeside Avenue*

The site includes the home and the laboratory buildings where inventor Thomas Alva Edison lived and worked the last 44 years of his life. Erected in 1887, the laboratory complex, with its teams of workers, became the prototype for the modern industrial research laboratory. Today the buildings contain exhibits that include Edison's original tinfoil photograph, the first motion-picture camera and other movie apparatus, and early electric light and power equipment. There is also a replica of the "Black Maria," the world's first motion-picture studio. **Glenmont**, Edison's 23-room home, contains almost all the

original furnishings as well as gifts from well-known people all over the world. The graves of Edison and his wife are behind the house.
Lab open Wed-Sun 9:30—3. House closed until 1986.

NEW MEXICO

ACOMA NATIONAL HISTORIC LANDMARK, *13 miles south of Casa Blanca on State 23*

Established about 1300, Acoma pueblo is believed to be the oldest continuously occupied settlement in the nation. In 1540 a detachment of soldiers led by Hernando de Alvarado from the Coronado expedition into New Mexico became the first Europeans to discover this thriving community. From their strategically situated mesa top, 357 feet above the fields that they worked below, the Indians of Acoma successfully resisted the Spanish for nearly a century, until the numerical superiority of the conquistadors forced them to surrender. The Franciscans founded the **San Estevan de Rey Mission** (NHL) at Acoma in 1629; it is in use today. A few families still live in the adobe houses at Acoma, and other Indians convene here for periodic festivals when it is closed to visitors.
Open: daily, 1 hour after sunrise–1 hour before sunset

SANTA FE AND VICINITY

BARRIO DE ANALCO HISTORIC DISTRICT NATIONAL HISTORIC LANDMARK

One of the nation's oldest European settlements, this barrio, or district, was founded in the 1620s across the Santa Fe River from the side of town where prominent officials and citizens lived. Characterized by numerous examples of adobe construction, which merged Indian and Spanish building styles, the barrio continues to be an active working-class neighborhood.

PALACE OF THE GOVERNORS NATIONAL HISTORIC LANDMARK, *north side of the plaza*

The oldest public building in the United States was erected in 1610 by Governor Pedro de Peralta, who established Santa Fe as the capital of the Spanish Southwest. The building served as the Spanish seat of government for more than 2 centuries, except for the period of the Pueblo Rebellion of 1680, when the palace was seized by Indians and occupied until the reconquest in 1693. In 1821 the Mexican government took over the palace for official business. General Stephen Watts Kearny raised the American flag at the building during the Mexican War of 1846. It subsequently housed 22 U.S. territorial governors. Today the palace has been restored and contains a museum devoted to the history of New Mexico.
Open: Mar-Sept, daily 9–4:45; rest of the year, closed Mondays

SANTA FE PLAZA NATIONAL HISTORIC LANDMARK

This historical heart of Santa Fe, founded as the Spanish capital of New Mexico in 1610 and the oldest seat of government in the United States, was the terminus of the **Old Santa Fe Trail**. The plaza is associated with such landmarks as the **Palace of the Governors** *(see)* and the nearby **Mission of San Miguel,** which was begun in 1610 and is one of the oldest churches in the country.
Mission of San Miguel open daily 9–11:30, 1–4:30, closed Wednesday

TAOS

TAOS PUEBLO NATIONAL HISTORIC LANDMARK, *3 miles north*
Built by the Tigua Indians, these 5-story communal dwellings—the tallest pueblo buildings in the Southwest—recall Indian resistance to Spanish rule during the 1600s. Spanish explorers had visited Taos Pueblo as early as 1540. Erected about 1598 near the entrance to the pueblo, the **Mission of San Geronimo** was destroyed and rebuilt twice before the Indian uprising of 1680. After reconquest, in 1694, the mission was reestablished and continued to operate until 1847, when it was bombarded by American troops under Colonel Sterling Price during the Taos Rebellion. Only ruins of the mission remain. Taos Pueblo still houses about 1,800 Indians.

Acoma's lofty perch protected its inhabitants until 1598, when Juan de Oñate's Spanish troops scaled the rocky walls.

HARVEY CAPLIN

NEW YORK

HYDE PARK

HOME OF FRANKLIN D. ROOSEVELT NATIONAL HISTORIC SITE, *U.S. 9*

President Franklin D. Roosevelt was born in this beautiful frame house which was his home throughout his lifetime. During his years as president it was known as the Summer White House. The historic site also includes the **Roosevelt Library and Museum** and the grave sites of the President and Mrs. Roosevelt. Accessible by bus from here is the **Eleanor Roosevelt Historic Site**. Her cottage "Val-Kill" has been restored as it was when she lived here.

FDR Home open: May-Oct, daily 9–5:30; Nov-Apr, daily 9–4:30; Jan-Feb, closed Tues and Wed. Eleanor Roosevelt site open: Mar-Nov, daily 9–5

VANDERBILT MANSION NATIONAL HISTORIC SITE, *U.S. 9*

Called the symbol of an era, this magnificent 54-room Italian Renaissance palace is representative of the grand estates built by America's industrial millionaires in the post-Civil War years. Frederick W. Vanderbilt, grandson of the "commodore," had his mansion built in 1896 by McKim, Mead & White, the nation's foremost architects.

Open: May-Oct, daily 9–5:30; Nov-Apr, daily 9–4:30; Jan-Feb, closed Tues-Wed

NEW YORK CITY, BROOKLYN

BROOKLYN BRIDGE NATIONAL HISTORIC LANDMARK

A landmark famous the world over for its beauty and design, this bridge was one of the first woven-wire cable suspension bridges ever constructed. Designed by John A. Roebling, the bridge spanned 1,595 feet between Manhattan and the city of Brooklyn and was opened in 1883 after 13 years of construction. Its design and execution, considered a marvel of engineering, were so outstanding that it was 50 years before a significantly longer bridge was built and 70 years before major reinforcements were required.

NEW YORK CITY, MANHATTAN

CASTLE CLINTON NATIONAL MONUMENT, *Battery Park*

Built in 1811 as part of the defenses of New York City in the imminent war with Great Britain, this fort served a variety of purposes. It was a U.S. military post until 1821, when it was ceded to New York City, which in turn leased it as a place for public entertainment. As **Castle Garden** the fort was the scene of outstanding events such as a reception for Lafayette in 1824 and the American debut of Jenny Lind in 1850. Five years later Castle Garden was converted to an immigrant landing depot. Between 1855 and 1889, when the depot closed, nearly 8 million immigrants passed through. From 1896 until 1941 the **New York City Aquarium** was housed here.

Open Mar-Nov, daily 9–5; Dec-Feb, Thurs-Mon 9–4:30

CENTRAL PARK NATIONAL HISTORIC LANDMARK, *from 59th to 110th streets and from Fifth Avenue to Central Park West*

The 840 acres of landscaped wooded grounds was completed in 1876 according to the inspired designs of Frederick Law Olmsted and Calvert Vaux. The plans of the original roadways for horses and carriages and pedestrian walks have never had to be changed to

After it opened its doors in 1891, three-quarters of all newcomers passed through the Ellis Island immigration station.

LIBRARY OF CONGRESS

accommodate the motorcar and the expanded population of the 20th century. The lakes, skating rinks, bandstands, carousel, zoos, free Shakespearean theater, and flower gardens are a few of the attractions that delight the visitor in Central Park.

CITY HALL NATIONAL HISTORIC LANDMARK, *City Hall Park, Broadway and Chambers St*

The seat of city government, an architectural masterpiece designed by John McComb and Joseph Mangin and built in 1802-12, combines a French classical plan with Federal details. The Declaration of Independence was read to the colonial army near this site on July 9, 1776.

Open: Mon–Fri 9–4

COOPER UNION NATIONAL HISTORIC LANDMARK, *Fourth Avenue and Seventh Street*

In 1857 Peter Cooper, manufacturer, inventor, and philanthropist, founded Cooper Union, an educational institution "for the advancement of science and art." A pioneer in free public education, Cooper Union offered a unique curriculum of general science combined with practical training. Spokesmen for many important issues addressed audiences here, and from this podium on February 27, 1860, Abraham Lincoln launched his campaign for the presidential nomination.

ELLIS ISLAND NATIONAL HISTORIC SITE, *New York Harbor*

For more than 16 million immigrants, Ellis Island was the last stop on the journey to America and a new life. The Island functioned as the principal port of entry for immigrants beginning in 1892 and was abruptly closed in 1954. Presently undergoing restoration, the historic site is expected to reopen in 1986.

FEDERAL HALL NATIONAL MEMORIAL, *Nassau and Wall streets*

The nation's first Capitol, Federal Hall was the site of the meeting of the first Congress and the swearing-in of George Washington as the first President on April 30, 1789. Built in 1703 as city hall, the building witnessed many famous events: the landmark trial of John Peter Zenger for freedom of the press, the meeting of the Stamp Act Congress of 1765, and the meetings of the government under the Articles of Confederation. When Congress moved to Philadelphia, Federal Hall fell into disrepair and was sold for salvage. The present structure, now a museum, was built in 1842 as a custom-house and subtreasury building. A statue dedicated in 1883 by Grover Cleveland celebrates Washington's inauguration.
Open Mon-Fri, 9–5

FRAUNCES TAVERN, *54 Pearl Street*

This building is a 1907 replica of the one Etienne de Lancey built in 1719. Originally his private residence, the house was converted to a tavern in 1763 by Samuel Fraunces. Here, 20 years later, George Washington delivered his famous farewell address to his officers. The tavern is now a restaurant and museum of the Revolution.
Open Mon-Fri 10–4

GENERAL GRANT NATIONAL MEMORIAL, *Riverside Drive and West 122nd Street*

This 150-foot gray granite monument overlooking the Hudson River was built as a memorial to Ulysses S. Grant, supreme commander of the Union armies and 18th President of the United States. Familiarly known as Grant's Tomb, the memorial has exhibits relating to Grant's life and the Civil War.
Open Wed-Sun 9–5

HAMILTON GRANGE NATIONAL MEMORIAL, *287 Convent Avenue*

Alexander Hamilton, first Secretary of the Treasury and a proponent of Federalism, lived in this house for the last 3 years of his life. A restoration program is in progress.
Open Wed-Sun 9–5

STATUE OF LIBERTY NATIONAL MONUMENT, *Liberty Island*

This colossal statue standing in New York Harbor has come to symbolize all that is good in America to millions of people around the world. Dedicated in 1886 by President Grover Cleveland, the statue

was designed by Frédéric Auguste Bartholdi as a gift to the United States from the people of France to commemorate the alliance of friendship between the two countries. The famous poem at the base was written by Emma Lazarus. Parts of the Statue are closed for restoration until 1986. The Museum of Immigration remains open.
Museum open Wed-Sun 10:15–4

UNITED NATIONS HEADQUARTERS, *42 East 48th Street at First Avenue*

The United Nations was created in 1945 as an instrument of world peace and unity. The headquarters occupies 18 acres along the East River and was the work of the world's leading architects.
Open daily 9:15–4:45

OYSTER BAY, LONG ISLAND

SAGAMORE HILL NATIONAL HISTORIC SITE, *Cove Neck Road*

Built as a summer residence by Theodore Roosevelt in 1884–85, this house soon became his permanent home. From 1901, when he assumed the Presidency on the death of William McKinley, until 1909, Sagamore Hill served as the Summer White House, and it was here on January 6, 1919, that Roosevelt died.
Open daily 9–5

TICONDEROGA

FORT TICONDEROGA NATIONAL HISTORIC LANDMARK, *1 mile northeast on State 73*

Because of its strategic location at the junction of Lakes George and Champlain, this outpost was a cornerstone of the defense of Canada and the Hudson River Valley. The French built star-shaped **Fort Carillon** in 1755, and Montcalm won a major battle here in 1758; but they abandoned it to the British the following year. During the Revolution the post changed hands many times, first falling to the Americans in May 1775, when Ethan Allen and his Green Mountain Boys captured it. In 1777 it was retaken by the British and destroyed. The restored fort features an outstanding museum.
Open: May 15-June, daily 8–6; July-Aug, daily 8–7; Sept-Oct 15, daily 8–6

WEST POINT

UNITED STATES MILITARY ACADEMY NATIONAL HISTORIC LANDMARK

Since 1802, when the Academy was established by Congress, West Point has trained officers for the regular Army. Because of its commanding position above the Hudson River, General Washington insisted that a regular garrison be stationed here, and in 1778 defenses were constructed under the direction of Thaddeus Kosciusko, America's outstanding Polish ally. In 1780 an attempt was made by Benedict Arnold, then commander of the post, to betray the Point, but his plot was uncovered in time. Earlier in the Revolution a chain was strung across the Hudson to block passage of the British fleet; some links from that chain can be seen near **Battle Monument**, a memorial to regular Army men killed during the Civil War.

The Brooklyn Bridge well under way: the towers are finished, and half the deck is already hung from the great suspension cables.

MUSEUM OF THE CITY OF NEW YORK

NORTH CAROLINA

ASHEVILLE AND VICINITY

BILTMORE ESTATES NATIONAL HISTORIC LANDMARK, *2 miles south on U.S. 25*

The 19th-century French Renaissance mansion built here for George W. Vanderbilt is now a museum of art treasures and historic objects. The gardens were designed by Frederick Law Olmsted.

Open daily 9–5

KITTY HAWK

WRIGHT BROTHERS NATIONAL MEMORIAL, *Kill Devil Hills*

On December 17, 1903, the Wright brothers, Orville and Wilbur, launched the first successful flight of a power-driven passenger-carrying airplane. Though the craft was in the air only about 12 seconds and traveled but 120 feet, the event was historic in the most literal sense: it proved the possibility of aviation and spurred a wholly new means of travel. In addition to the memorial itself, there are markers that indicate the takeoff and landing spots. There is also a reproduction of the 1903 craft and structures, representing the Wrights' camp as they prepared for the flight.

Open daily 9–5; hours extended in summer

NEW BERN

TRYON PALACE, *George Street between Eden and Metcalf streets*

Built between 1767 and 1770 and largely destroyed by fire in 1798, this magnificent colonial mansion, now restored, was built for William Tryon, royal governor of North Carolina. It also served as the first state capitol (until 1794). The Tryon complex includes the **John Wright Stanly House**, completed in the 1780s by Stanly, merchant and patriot, and visited by Washington, Lafayette, and Nathanael Greene.

Open: Mon-Sat 9:30–4, Sun 1:30–4

ROANOKE ISLAND, MANTEO VICINITY

FORT RALEIGH NATIONAL HISTORIC SITE, *4 miles north on U.S. 158*

This is the scene of the earliest English attempts to establish colonies within the present limits of the United States. With a patent to explore the New World, Sir Walter Raleigh sponsored the first of 2 settlements on this site in 1585. This did not prosper, in part because of difficulties with Indians, in part because the colonists' main activity was directed more toward locating riches than toward establishing a new home. They returned to England in 1586 with the aid of Sir Francis Drake, leaving behind a small detachment to hold the fort. But when an enlarged company under Raleigh's patronage returned to Roanoke Island in 1587, those who had remained could not be found. This was the beginning of a series of mysteries surrounding the second colonization attempt, which resulted in the so-called Lost Colony. It was here that Virginia Dare became the first child born of English parents in the New World. The going proved difficult again, and Governor John White returned to England for help later in 1587. But England's preoccupation with the threat of a Spanish invasion made it impossible to obtain aid for the colony; when White returned in 1591, he "found the houses taken down and the place very strongly enclosed with a high palisade of great trees, with curtains and

With Orville at the controls and Wilbur running alongside, the Wright brothers bring the world into the air age, December 17, 1903.

LIBRARY OF CONGRESS

flankers, very fortlike." The fate of the 116 settlers of the Lost Colony was never determined. But historical records of Fort Raleigh, constructed by the colonists and rebuilt by the second contingent of 1587, and subsequent archaeological evidence have made possible reconstruction of the original earth fort. Within the present 144-acre area there are portions of the settlement sites of both 1585 and 1587. Other points of interest are an **Elizabethan Garden** and a visitor center. *Park open sunrise to sunset. Visitor center open: June-Aug, daily 9–8; rest of year, daily 9–5.*

WINSTON-SALEM

OLD SALEM HISTORIC DISTRICT NATIONAL HISTORIC LANDMARK

The town of Salem was founded in 1766 by a Moravian colony and was consolidated with Winston in 1913. Now authentically restored, Old Salem is an outstanding example of an 18th-century German community. The more than 30 restored structures include **Salem Tavern** (NHL), built in 1784 and visited by George Washington in 1791, and **Single Brothers House** (NHL), erected in 1768–69 (and enlarged in 1786) of German half-shingle construction as a dwelling for unmarried males over 14.
Open: weekdays 9:30–4:30, Sun 1–4:30

NORTH DAKOTA

MEDORA AND VICINITY

THEODORE ROOSEVELT NATIONAL PARK, *headquarters in Medora*

Though primarily noted for its natural beauty, this 70,000-acre park in the Badlands has an important historical association. Theodore Roosevelt came to the area in 1883, first to hunt and then to ranch for a 4-year period. Two Roosevelt ranches were on the site—the **Maltese Cross** and **Elkhorn**—and the park preserves the locale of the headquarters of his Elkhorn Ranch. The park is a memorial to his work in behalf of conservation.

Visitor center open daily 8–4:30; hours extended in summer

OHIO

CHILLICOTHE VICINITY

MOUND CITY GROUP NATIONAL MONUMENT, *4 miles north on State 104*

This area was the cultural center of one of the most remarkable prehistoric civilizations in the Americas—that of the Indians now called Hopewell. Much of southern Ohio has a Hopewellian legacy; this site is among the most famous localities where excavation (begun here in 1846) has produced a wealth of artifacts. The site contains 24 burial mounds within a 13-acre earthen enclosure. The remains date from 200 B.C. to A.D. 500.

Visitor center open: June-Labor Day, 8–8; rest of year, 8–5

LOCUST GROVE VICINITY

SERPENT MOUND NATIONAL HISTORIC LANDMARK, *4 miles northwest on State 73*

The Great Serpent Mound, occupying a hill crest parallel to Brush Creek, is the largest serpent effigy mound in the United States, nearly a quarter mile in length. It was also one of the first areas to be set aside because of its prehistoric associations and scientific value. Excavations have determined the plan of its construction by the Adena Indians between 1000 B.C. to A.D. 700.

Museum open: Memorial Day-Oct, Mon-Sat 9:30–5, Sun 12–5

OKLAHOMA

CLEO SPRINGS VICINITY

HOMESTEADER'S SOD HOUSE, *4 miles north on State 8*

Erected in 1894 by Marshall McCully, who came to Oklahoma during the great land rush of 1893, this structure is the only extant original homesteader sod house in the state. The house now contains furnishings typical of 1907, the year Oklahoma achieved statehood.

Open: Tues-Fri 9–5, Sat-Sun 2–5

OREGON

ASTORIA AND VICINITY

FORT ASTORIA NATIONAL HISTORIC LANDMARK, *Fifteenth and Exchange streets*

In 1811 John Jacob Astor, founder of the Pacific Fur Trading Company, sponsored an expedition to the Columbia River in an attempt to

break the British fur trading monopoly. The "Astorians" erected an outpost at this site, the first white settlement in the Oregon Country. During the War of 1812 rumors of an attack by British men-of-war caused the post to be abandoned. Fort Astoria was restored to the United States in 1815, and it subsequently played an important role in the settlement of Oregon. Today a portion of Fort Astoria has been reconstructed.
Open daily

PENNSYLVANIA

EPHRATA

EPHRATA CLOISTER NATIONAL HISTORIC LANDMARK, *junction of U.S. 322 and 222*

Led by Johann Conrad Beissel, a group of Seventh-Day German Baptists settled this town about 1730 as a communal, semimonastic religious society. The religious orders were virtually extinct by the end of the 18th century, but the society's buildings, known as Ephrata Cloister, were occupied by members until about 1934. Still standing are the **Saal**, constructed in 1740 as a community house; **Saron**, or Sisters' House, 1742–43; Beissel's log dwelling; the **Almonry**, or alms and bake house; an academy dating from 1837; and cottages.
Open: Tues-Sat 9–5, Sun 12–5

Ephrata Cloister, Pennsylvania, was founded by Seventh-Day German Baptists in about 1730.

PENNSYLVANIA HISTORICAL AND MUSEUM COLLECTION, HARRISBURG, PENNA.

GETTYSBURG

GETTYSBURG NATIONAL MILITARY PARK, *visitor center on State 134*

Seeking a decisive victory here on Northern soil, the Confederate forces of General Robert E. Lee received instead a setback from which they never fully recovered. The battle, July 1–3, 1863, pitted Lee's Army of Northern Virginia against the Army of the Potomac, commanded by Major General George G. Meade. Thirty miles of road traverse areas of the park where fighting occurred in this famous battle, which turned the tide of the Civil War; along the way are more than 1,400 monuments, statues, and markers, and three observation towers. Within the park is the site where Lincoln delivered the Gettysburg Address on November 19, 1863, to dedicate nearby **Gettysburg National Cemetery**. Guided tours are available, and among other noteworthy locales are the **Eternal Light Peace Memorial**, **Meade's Headquarters**, the **High Water Mark Monument**, and **Devil's Den** (a Confederate stronghold). Outside the park are the **National Civil War Wax Museum**, the **Gettysburg National Museum**, the **Hall of Presidents**, and the **Lincoln Room Museum**. On the southwest edge of the park is **Eisenhower National Historic Site**, the general's farm where he lived until his death.

Visitor center open daily 8–5. Eisenhower home open: Apr-Nov, daily 9–5, Dec-Mar, closed Mon-Tues

PHILADELPHIA

AMERICAN PHILOSOPHICAL SOCIETY HALL NATIONAL HISTORIC LANDMARK, *Independence Square*

The brick building, now restored, dates from 1789. The society whose home this is traces its origin to 1768. Benjamin Franklin was the first president of the organization, which is the oldest learned society in the United States.

ARCH STREET MEETINGHOUSE, *302–338 Arch Street*

Dating from 1804, this is the city's oldest meetinghouse of the Society of Friends. It was built on land given by William Penn and first used as a cemetery.

BARTRAM HOUSE NATIONAL HISTORIC LANDMARK, *54th Street and Eastwick Avenue*

The home of John Bartram (1699–1777), pioneer American botanist, stands here amid his even more famous gardens, where he cultivated rare and exotic plants. The stone structure was built in 1731 and is now furnished with period pieces.

Open: Apr-Oct, Tues-Sun 10–4; Nov-Mar, Tues-Fri 10–4

CARPENTERS' HALL NATIONAL HISTORIC LANDMARK, *320 Chestnut Street*

Included in Independence National Historic Park *(see)*, this brick structure was built in 1770 as a guildhall by the Carpenters' Company, which still owns and maintains it. The First Continental Congress met there in September, 1774.

Open: Tues-Sun, 10–4

CHRIST CHURCH NATIONAL HISTORIC LANDMARK, *Second Street between Market and Filbert streets*

George Washington and Benjamin Franklin were among the notables who worshiped at this church, built between 1727 and 1754. The

Georgian colonial building is an outstanding example of church architecture of the period. The church burial grounds at Fifth and Arch streets contain the graves of Franklin and his wife, Deborah. The church is part of Independence National Historical Park.
Open daily 9–5; Sun services at 9 and 11

CONGRESS HALL, *Sixth and Chestnut streets*
Built between 1787 and 1789 as the Philadelphia County Courthouse, this brick structure served as the meeting place of the U.S. Congress from 1790 to 1800. It was the scene of George Washington's second inaugural address and his Farewell Address, and of John Adams' induction as second President of the United States. It is part of Independence National Historical Park.
Open daily 9–5

DESHLER-MORRIS HOUSE, *5442 Germantown Avenue*
President George Washington resided here briefly during the summers of 1793 and 1794, when yellow fever forced the government to move out of the main part of Philadelphia. It is included in Independence National Historical Park.
Open: Apr-Dec, Tues-Sun 1–4; closed holidays

ELFRETH'S ALLEY HISTORIC DISTRICT NATIONAL HISTORIC LANDMARK, *between Second and Front streets*
This oldest unchanged and continuously occupied street in the city is an authentic slice of colonial Philadelphia, containing 17th- and 18th-century workingmen's homes and a museum.
Museum open: daily 10–4

FIRST BANK OF THE UNITED STATES, *116 South Third Street*
Erected between 1795 and 1797, this is thought to be the oldest bank building in the United States. Now part of Independence National Historic Park.

GLORIA DEI (OLD SWEDES') CHURCH NATIONAL HISTORIC SITE, *Swanson Street between Christian and Water streets*
This oldest existing church building in Philadelphia was constructed between 1698 and 1700 by Swedish colonists. Still in active service, it is also of great interest architecturally.
Open by appointment

INDEPENDENCE NATIONAL HISTORIC PARK, *bounded by Walnut, Sixth, Chestnut, and Second streets*
Independence Hall, at Sixth and Chestnut streets, is the principal gem of the collection of historic treasures located within this district. Constructed between 1732 and 1756 as the Pennsylvania State House, it is the home of the Liberty Bell; here, on July 4, 1776, the Declaration of Independence was adopted, a year following the gathering of the Second Continental Congress in the same building, and it was here in 1787 that the Constitutional Convention presided over by Washington created the U.S. Constitution. Here, too, in 1775, Washington accepted the post of Commander in Chief of the American Army. Independence Park components, not all situated within the area indicated above, also include the First Bank of the United States, Carpenters' Hall, American Philosophical Society Hall, Congress Hall, Christ Church, Gloria Dei Church, and the Deshler-Morris House (all of which are described separately in this section), together with the **Second Bank of the United States**,

Library Hall, **Old City Hall** (used by the U.S. Supreme Court from 1791 to 1800), the **Bishop White House**, **St. Joseph's Church**, **St. George's Church**, and **Mikveh Israel Cemetery**.
Independence Hall and visitor center on Walnut St. open daily 9–5

UNIONTOWN VICINITY

FORT NECESSITY NATIONAL BATTLEFIELD, *11 miles east on U.S. 40*

Here, on July 3, 1754, the French and Indians forced the surrender of colonial troops commanded by Lieutenant Colonel George Washington in the opening engagement of the French and Indian War. Reconstructions of the fort's stockade and entrenchments have been made on their original sites. Also here are **Mount Washington Tavern**, built around 1818 and now a museum, and the grave of General Edward Braddock, who was killed in 1755 in another engagement with the French. Jumonville Glen, a detached part of the park located 7 miles to the northwest, was the site of a skirmish prior to the battle of Fort Necessity.
Visitor center open daily 8:30–5; Fort open: May-Oct, daily 9–6; Nov-Apr, daily 10–5

VALLEY FORGE NATIONAL HISTORICAL PARK LANDMARK

Suffering from hardship, hunger, and a succession of defeats, the army commanded by General George Washington arrived at the scene of this historic encampment on December 19, 1777. Though the winter was a bitter one, the army emerged in the spring as a rejuvenated force capable of coping with British regulars. Remains of trenches and earthworks are visible, along with the restored soldiers' huts. Other attractions of the park are the stone house used by Washington as his headquarters, General Varnum's quarters, and the encampment parade ground. Special tours and activities are available during the travel season; tours begin at the Visitor Center.
Open daily 8:30–5

RHODE ISLAND

NEWPORT

NEWPORT HISTORIC DISTRICT NATIONAL HISTORIC LANDMARK, *bounded by Van Zandt Avenue, Farewell, Sherman, High, Thomas, Golden Hill, Thames, Marsh, and Washington streets*

Built at the height of Newport's prosperity as a seaport, these mid-18th-century public and private structures represent the most advanced examples of academic Georgian architecture produced in the colonies. Many of the buildings reflect the work of the master carpenter Richard Munday or the distinguished architect Peter Harrison. Completed by Munday in 1742, the **Old Colony House** (NHL) initially housed the general assembly of Rhode Island colony; on July 20, 1776, the acceptance of the Declaration was read from its balcony, and during the Revolution George Washington attended a banquet in the great hall with the Comte de Rochambeau; the Federal Constitution was ratified at the building in 1790, and the state legislature met here from 1790 until 1900. The **Brick Market** (NHL), a commercial edifice with an open arcade on the ground floor, was built by Harrison between 1762 and 1772 and was used at various times as a theater and as a town and city hall. Another era of Newport's history is recalled in the **Bellevue Avenue Historic District National Historic Landmark**

This teeming interior is a small section of the Breakers, the gargantuan Vanderbilt home in Newport, Rhode Island

PRESERVATION SOCIETY OF NEWPORT COUNTY, NEWPORT, R.I.

and the **Ocean Drive Newport Historic District National Historic Landmark**, where the "summer cottages" that made this resort world-famous can be seen. Among the many mansions open to the public are **The Elms** (1901), **Marble House** (1892), **The Breakers** (1895), and **Hammersmith Farm** (1887).

SOUTH CAROLINA

CHARLESTON AND VICINITY

FORT MOULTRIE, *West Middle Street, Sullivan's Island*

The first fort, one of three built on this site, was constructed of palmetto logs and sand. It was the scene of an important Revolutionary War battle on June 28, 1776, when 360 soldiers under Colonel William Moultrie defeated a fleet of 9 English warships and forestalled British occupation of the South. In 1793 the new nation moved to protect its shores with the first nationwide system of coastal defense. As a result of this program, a second Fort Moultrie was built to replace the first fort, which had fallen to ruins. In 1804 the second Fort Moultrie was destroyed by a hurricane. By 1909 the third Fort Moultrie had been constructed as part of the second system of coastal forts for the United States. This fort was altered many times during years of rapidly changing technology, eventually becoming just a small part of the Fort Moultrie reservations stretching over much of Sullivan's Island. The fort was deactivated in 1947. Today it has been restored to display each of the major periods of its use, telling the story of U.S. seacoast defense from 1776 to 1947. It is now part of the Fort Sumter National Monument.

Open Apr-Oct, daily 9–6; Nov-Mar, daily 9–5

FORT SUMTER NATIONAL MONUMENT, *Charleston Harbor*

Begun in 1829 as part of the third system of coastal forts, Fort Sumter was nearing completion when South Carolina seceded from the Union in December 1860. Fearing attack from the secessionists, the small Federal garrison at Fort Moultrie evacuated to Fort Sumter. For over three months the garrison held out. Finally, on April 12, 1861, after all negotiations had failed. Confederate forces opened fire on Fort Sumter. After 34 hours of bombardment the garrison of the fort surrendered and a nation was plunged into civil war. When the Confederates evacuated the fort 4 years later, it was little more than a mass of rubble. For 20 months Fort Sumter and Fort Moultrie had been pounded by Union ironclads and shore batteries, yet the defenses of Charleston Harbor held. They yielded only after Sherman's army had captured the capital of Columbia. Fort Sumter, like Fort Moultrie, went through several periods of modernization, remaining part of the seacoast defenses until 1947. The following year the fort was declared a national monument. Today much of the fort has been excavated and there is a museum on the site. Tour boats to the fort leave from downtown Charleston.

For further information write: 1214 Middle St., Sullivan's Island, SC 29482

SITE OF OLD CHARLES TOWNE, *State 171, on the west bank of the Ashley River*

The site of the state's first permanent settlement is now a historic park. In April 1670 a colony of English settlers was established at Albemarle Point, due west of the city's present location, and named

On April 12, 1861, Confederate forces fired the shot against Fort Sumter that began the Civil War.

SOUTH CAROLINA DEPARTMENT OF PARKS AND RECREATION

Charles Towne in honor of King Charles II. As part of the South Carolina tricentennial in 1970, a 200-acre site was developed to include the original 10-acre area of the colony, complete with reconstructed stockade, redoubt, and trenches. Across the Ashley, a section of old Charleston noted for its architectural value forms Charleston Historic District (NHL). The magnificent Georgian and Federal town mansions reflect the great wealth that Charlestonians amassed before the Revolution from rice and indigo plantations and from cotton thereafter.

SOUTH DAKOTA

KEYSTONE VICINITY

MOUNT RUSHMORE NATIONAL MEMORIAL, *3 miles west off U.S. 16A*

Carved in the granite of Mount Rushmore are likenesses of the heads of 4 American Presidents: George Washington, Thomas Jefferson, Abraham Lincoln, and Theodore Roosevelt; each between 60 and 70 feet in height. They are the work of the sculptor Gutzon Borglum. The memorial is best viewed under morning light; from Memorial Day to Labor Day, floodlights are used at night, and evening programs in the amphitheater recount the philosophies of the 4 Presidents and the history of the memorial project.

Open daily throughout the year

WOUNDED KNEE BATTLEFIELD NATIONAL HISTORIC LANDMARK, *on Pine Ridge Indian Reservation*

Historical markers and a mass grave containing the bodies of Chief Big Foot and more than a hundred of his Sioux followers mark the site of the last significant armed encounter between Indians and U.S. forces. Having been systematically deprived of their land and way of life, the Indians had turned in desperation to a "messiah craze," the principal ritual of which was a ghost dance, introduced by a Nevada Paiute named Wovoka. His vision of a land where the buffalo were restored and the white men driven out led to a religious fervor that swept through tribes in many parts of the West. Big Foot and his band of Sioux were on their way to a mass Indian revival gathering when the encounter occurred, December 29, 1890. U.S. troops overtook them; Big Foot seemed prepared to accept arrest, but he and his followers escaped, only to be overtaken again at Wounded Knee Creek. While they were disarming the Indians, resistance caused troops of the Seventh Cavalry to return the Sioux fire. The result was more a massacre than a battle. The poorly equipped Indians were soon routed, and those who fled were pursued and cut down. In the spring of 1973 Wounded Knee became a dramatic symbol of Indian dissatisfaction with their treatment by the U.S. government. A group of Indians occupied the town and were held under siege for 70 days by Federal marshals while they attempted to negotiate their grievances with government officials.

TENNESSEE

FORT DONELSON NATIONAL MILITARY PARK, *1 mile west of Dover on U.S. 79*

The first major Federal victory of the Civil War occurred at this site on the Cumberland River on February 16, 1862, when some 27,000 Union troops, aided by gunboats, under Ulysses S. Grant defeated approximately 18,000 Confederates. After 3 days of fighting, General Simon B. Buckner, the Confederate commander in charge, surrendered the stronghold in accordance with Grant's terms for an "unconditional and immediate surrender." The 14,000 Confederate prisoners of war turned over to the North represented the largest number of men ever to surrender at one time in North America. Grant's decisive victory dealt the Confederacy a mortal blow by opening 2 avenues into the heart of the South by way of the Tennessee and Cumberland rivers. The victory also raised flagging Union morale and made the nation aware of Grant's considerable military abilities. Preserved in this park are the earthworks of the fort, Confederate river batteries, a reconstructed powder magazine, 2 miles of trenches, and the Dover Hotel, where the surrender occurred. Adjacent to the site is the **Fort Donelson National Cemetery.** *For further information write: Superintendent, Dover, TN 37058*

NASHVILLE AND VICINITY

THE HERMITAGE NATIONAL HISTORIC LANDMARK, *12 miles east on U.S. 70N*

Andrew Jackson, who began his career as a frontier militia commander and became the nation's 7th President, built The Hermitage in 1819 and resided there until his death in 1845. In the Creek Indian War of 1813, Jackson earned a major general's commission and in 1815 became the hero of the Battle of New Orleans, the final

engagement of the War of 1812. Jackson served 2 terms as President (1829–37). He and his wife, Rachel, are buried at The Hermitage. Across the road stands **Tulip Grove**, a plantation house erected in 1836 by Mrs. Jackson's nephew, Andrew Jackson Donelson.
Open daily 9–5

SHILOH NATIONAL MILITARY PARK, *10 miles south of Savannah and Adamsville, via U.S. 64 and 22*

The first major western engagement of the Civil War occurred at this site on April 6–7, 1862. After the fall of Forts Henry and Donelson *(see Fort Donelson National Military Park)*, Confederate General Albert Sidney Johnston withdrew his troops from Kentucky and most of Tennessee and concentrated about 40,000 men at Corinth, Mississippi. Grant pursued Johnston and stopped with approximately 40,000 men at **Pittsburgh Landing**, 23 miles north of Corinth, to await reinforcements led by General Don Carlos Buell. Johnston decided to thwart Grant's plan by attacking the Federals at the site of **Shiloh Church** on April 6. Johnston was mortally wounded at the **Peach Orchard** and was succeeded in command by General P. G. T. Beauregard. That night Buell's army arrived and increased Grant's force to almost 62,000 men. The next day Grant launched a counterattack and finally forced the Southerners to retreat unpursued to Corinth. The Union victory was an important milestone in the campaign aimed at securing control of the Mississippi River, and it directly led to the capture of Corinth by the Federals that May. The Union dead were buried at the adjoining **Shiloh (Pittsburgh Landing) National Cemetery**.
For further information write: Superintendent, Shiloh, TN 38376

TEXAS

JOHNSON CITY AND VICINITY

LYNDON B. JOHNSON NATIONAL HISTORICAL PARK, *15 miles west in Stonewall off U.S. 290 on Park Road 49*

This site in the Texas hill country includes the **Birthplace** and **Boyhood Home** of Lyndon Baines Johnson, 36th President of the United States. The son of Sam Ealy Johnson, Jr., a Texas legislator, and Rebekah Baines Johnson was born in a 2-bedroom farmhouse on the banks of the Pedernales River in 1908. When Lyndon was 5, his parents moved to a Victorian frame house in nearby Johnson City to provide a better education for their children. Lyndon lived here until his graduation from high school in 1924. After an active political career as congressman (1937–49), senator (1949–60), Vice-President (1960–63), and President (1963–69), Johnson retired to the LBJ ranch near his birthplace. After his death in 1973, Johnson was buried in a family plot beside the Pedernales. The site is divided into two sections: the **Johnson City Unit** contains the restored boyhood home, and the **Johnson Settlement**, including the log house owned by the president's grandfather. The **LBJ Ranch Unit**, located on the LBJ Ranch, is accessible only by bus tour from LBJ State Historical Park. Here is a reconstruction of his birthplace, his gravesite, and the one-room schoolhouse he attended. Both houses are shown with Johnson family memorabilia.
Open daily 9–5. Tours to the LBJ Ranch, daily 10–4. For further information write: Box 329, Johnson City, TX 78636

KINGSVILLE VICINITY

KING RANCH NATIONAL HISTORIC LANDMARK, *west off State 141*

The largest and best-known ranch in the continental United States was founded early in 1850s by Captain Richard King, who purchased a 75,000-acre tract, one of the original Spanish land grants, on Santa Gertrudis Creek. Here was developed the Santa Gertrudis breed of cattle, the first strain to originate in the Western Hemisphere. Today the ranch has grown to more than 1,250,000 acres. A 12-mile loop drive passes ranch headquarters, stables, and other interesting sights.
Drive open daily 9–5

SAN ANTONIO

THE ALAMO NATIONAL HISTORIC LANDMARK, *Alamo Plaza*

Originally known as Mission San Antonio de Valero, San Antonio's earliest mission was established in 1718 and converted into a fortress after 1793. The Alamo was the scene of the famous Texas Revolution battle of March 6, 1836, in which a force of 188 Americans under Colonel William B. Travis was slaughtered by Santa Anna's Mexican Army of 5,000. Texas had declared its independence from Mexico in 1836, and the group under Travis, including Colonel James Bowie and Davy Crockett, took a "victory or death" oath to defend San Antonio to the last man. The Mexican army began its siege of the Alamo on February 24. After repeated assaults, the walls of the Alamo were finally scaled on March 6, and all the defenders were massacred. Not only did the event cause Santa Anna many casualties and delay the Mexican invasion of Texas for 2 weeks, but it served to stiffen Texas resistance under the rallying cry "Remember the Alamo" and allowed the Texans to achieve victory that April at San Jacinto.
Open daily 9–5

SAN JOSE MISSION NATIONAL HISTORIC SITE, *6¼ miles south on U.S. 281*

San José y San Miguel de Aguayo was one of the most important missions on the northern frontier of New Spain during the 18th century. Founded in 1720 by Captain Juan Valdez, lieutenant general of the province of Texas, at the urging of Franciscan Fray Antonio Margíl de Jesus, the mission grew rapidly. By the middle of the 18th century San José was a thriving community with some 2,000 Indian convert residents caring for 3,000 head of livestock and producing 3,000 bushels of corn annually. Today San José is one of the best preserved examples of mission architecture.
For further information write: 6539 San Jose Dr., San Antonio, TX 78214

SPANISH GOVERNOR'S PALACE NATIONAL HISTORIC LANDMARK, *105 Military Plaza*

Constructed in 1749 to house commandants of the Presidio of Béxar, this aristocratic edifice after 1772 became headquarters of the Spanish government in Texas. In 1820 Moses Austin came to this building to secure the right to colonize Spanish Texas with U.S. citizens. The palace has been restored.
Open daily 9–5

The Alamo, our most celebrated mission, served as a stronghold for its ill-starred defenders during the Texas War for Independence.

SAN ANTONIO CONVENTION AND VISITOR'S BUREAU

LA VILLITA, *between South Presa and South Alamo streets*

The "little village" is an authentic restoration of San Antonio's earliest community, which was established by 1722 around the Mission San Antonio de Valero *(see San Antonio, the Alamo)*. Although the settlement was initially populated by poor Spanish soldiers and their Indian wives, La Villita became a fashionable residential district after 1819 when it was spared the ravages of a flood that destroyed most of San Antonio. One of the best-known adobe dwellings here belonged to General Perfecto de Cos, who at his home on December 9, 1835, signed the Articles of Capitulation after the Texans had captured San Antonio from the Mexicans. This humiliating incident probably influenced Cos' brother-in-law Santa Anna to spare no pity for the Texans at the Alamo in 1846, when he recaptured the town.

UTAH

SALT LAKE CITY AND VICINITY

BEEHIVE HOUSE, *75 East South Temple Street*

This Greek Revival mansion, surmounted with a beehive-shaped cupola—the traditional Mormon symbol of industry—was erected in 1854 for Brigham Young, president of the Mormon Church and first governor of the Utah Territory. In the mansion Young housed his large family and entertained prominent travelers and dignitaries of the day, including President Ulysses S. Grant. The building served as the official residence of presidents of the Mormon Church from 1893 until 1918.

Open: summer, Mon-Sat 9:30–4:30; winter, Mon-Sat 10–2:30

In 1897, to commemorate the fiftieth anniversary of their arrival in Utah, patriotic Mormons draped their Salt Lake City Temple.

SPECIAL COLLECTIONS, MARRIOTT LIBRARY, UNIVERSITY OF UTAH

TEMPLE SQUARE NATIONAL HISTORIC LANDMARK, *bounded by Main Street and North, West, and South Temple*

This walled square in the heart of Salt Lake City attests to the Mormon achievement of creating a "Kingdom of Zion" out of the Utah desert. On July 28, 1847, 4 days after his arrival in the Salt Lake Valley, Mormon leader Brigham Young came to this site between 2 forks of a small mountain stream and declared, "Here will be the temple of our God." The 10 acres composing Temple Square were marked off, and Salt Lake City soon grew up around the square. Dominating the area is the monumental gray granite **Temple**, which was designed by noted pioneer architect Truman O. Angell and took 40 years to erect (1853–93). The scene of sacred and secret Latter Day Saint ritual, the temple is closed to the public. Other edifices in Temple Square include the **Tabernacle**, completed in 1867, which boasts the world's largest domed roof, and the semi-Gothic **Assembly Hall**, raised in 1882. The **Sea Gull Monument** commemorates the summer of 1848, when hordes of crickets attacked the Mormon's crops; a flock of sea gulls providentially appeared and devoured the crickets. There are two visitor centers, one located at the north end and the other at the south end of the Square.

Open daily 8–10

VERMONT

SHELBURNE

S.S. *TICONDEROGA* NATIONAL HISTORIC LANDMARK, *Shelburne Museum, 7 miles south of Burlington on U.S. 7*

Launched in 1903, the steel-hulled S.S. *Ticonderoga* plied the waters of Lake Champlain until 1953 and is now the nation's only basically unaltered side-paddle-wheel steamboat. The former excursion boat is currently displayed in the **Shelburne Museum**, an outdoor museum of New England life over a span of 3 centuries.

Museum open: May 18-Oct 20, daily 9–5

VIRGINIA

ALEXANDRIA AND VICINITY

ALEXANDRIA HISTORIC DISTRICT NATIONAL HISTORIC LANDMARK

This district comprises nearly 100 blocks in the heart of the original town, which was established in 1748. George Washington was one of the surveyors of the district, which reflects Alexandria's position as the leading seaport and commercial center of northern Virginia for approximately 100 years, from about 1750 to the outset of the Civil War. Both historically and architecturally, many of the district's buildings merit close attention, among them:

GADSBY'S TAVERN NATIONAL HISTORIC LANDMARK, *128 North Royal Street*

This famous old inn, now restored, comprises 2 adjoining buildings erected in 1752 and 1792. Originally it was called City Tavern, and for many years it was both a social and a political center. Here, in 1754, George Washington set up an enrolling office for volunteers in his first command, and then a headquarters during the French and Indian War. From the tavern steps in 1799 he reviewed Alexandria troops in one of the last acts of his military career. John Paul Jones,

Lafayette, and Baron de Kalb are others who used the inn, located in the Alexandria Historic District.
Open daily

ROBERT E. LEE BOYHOOD HOME, *607 Oronoco Street*
The Georgian mansion here was the home of Robert E. Lee during 9 of his first 18 years. He was 5 when the Lee family moved into the house in 1812. Located within the Alexandria Historic District, the structure contains antiques and Lee memorabilia. Earlier the house was the scene of the courtship of George Washington Parke Custis, adopted grandson of George Washington, and Mary Fitzhugh. In 1831 the only child of that union, Mary Custis, became Mrs. Robert E. Lee.
Open: Mon-Sat 10–4, Sun 12–4; closed Dec 15-Jan

APPOMATTOX VICINITY

APPOMATTOX COURT HOUSE NATIONAL HISTORICAL PARK, *3 miles northeast on State 24*
To all intents, the Civil War ended here on April 9, 1865, with Lee's surrender of the Army of Northern Virginia to Grant. The long march to Appomattox had begun 7 days earlier for Lee's veteran but starving and badly outnumbered forces. Grant's cracking of the Richmond and Petersburg defense lines was followed by pursuit of Lee's army. Realizing that further combat would be in vain, Lee sought a meeting with Grant; the surrender took place in the **Wilmer McLean House**. This structure, dismantled in 1890, has now been reconstructed on its original site. The nearby courthouse also has been rebuilt, and other buildings in the area, including **Meeks General Store**, the **Woodson Law Office**, **Clover Hill Tavern**, the **County Jail**, and private homes, have been restored to their approximate 1865 appearance. The courthouse contains a museum and auditorium where audio-visual programs are presented.
Open: Sept-May, daily 8:30–5; June-Aug, daily 9–5:30

ARLINGTON VICINITY

ARLINGTON NATIONAL CEMETERY
Within Arlington National Cemetery are the graves of noted Americans, including Presidents Taft and Kennedy, Oliver Wendell Holmes, Generals John J. Pershing and George C. Marshall, and Admirals Robert E. Peary and Richard E. Byrd. Points of interest include the **Confederate Memorial**, **Marine Corps War Memorial**, and **Tomb of the Unknown Soldier**, containing the remains of veterans of the world wars and Korean conflict. On a hilltop site the **Custis-Lee Mansion**, also known as Arlington House, was constructed between 1802 and 1817 by George Washington Parke Custis, grandson of Martha Washington. His daughter, Mary Ann Randolph Custis, married Robert E. Lee here in 1831, and the house was the scene of most of their life together. The house and grounds were seized by Federal forces in 1861 in the move to fortify approaches to Washington, D.C. Four years later the area was converted into a national cemetery. The mansion is now the **Robert E. Lee Memorial** and contains some original furnishings, together with furnishings from Mount Vernon and personal effects of George Washington.
Arlington House open: Apr-Sept, daily 8–7; rest of year, daily 8–5

CHARLOTTESVILLE VICINITY

MONTICELLO NATIONAL HISTORIC LANDMARK, *2 miles south on State 53*

Not only was this the home of Thomas Jefferson for more than 50 years, it was virtually a lifetime project of his. It was built to his designs between 1769 and 1809, and its many inventive touches reveal his remarkable architectural skill. Richly furnished, the brick house in Roman Revival style contains many of his personal belongings. Jefferson is buried here.

Open: June-Aug, Mon-Fri 8–8, Sat, Sun 12–5; Sept-May, Mon-Fri 8–7, Sat, Sun 12–5

UNIVERSITY OF VIRGINIA, *university campus*

The university was founded by Thomas Jefferson in 1819 and designed by him as well. The focal point of his architectural plan was the **Rotunda** (NHL), adapted from the Pantheon in Rome and begun as the university library in 1822. It was destroyed by fire in 1895 and restored in 1898; meanwhile it had served as a banquet hall to honor Lafayette during a visit in 1824, and then as a Confederate military hospital. Extending southward from the Rotunda is the "academical village" of colonnades, arcades, faculty pavilions, and student dormitories, all part of the **University of Virginia Historic District** (NHL).

FREDERICKSBURG AND VICINITY

FREDERICKSBURG AND SPOTSYLVANIA COUNTY BATTLEFIELDS MEMORIAL NATIONAL MILITARY PARK, *Fredericksburg and the area in Spotsylvania County to the west and southwest*

The 3,672-acre park includes parts of 4 major Civil War battlefields (**Fredericksburg**, **Chancellorsville**, **the Wilderness**, and **Spotsylvania Court House**); **Fredericksburg National Cemetery**; the **Stonewall Jackson Memorial Shrine**, Guinea, Virginia (earlier Guiney's Station), the house in which Jackson died; and historic **Salem Church**. At Fredericksburg, December 11–13, 1862, General Ambrose E. Burnside's Army of the Potomac sought to dislodge Confederate forces under Lee from their entrenched positions on the heights west and south of the town. The attempt ended in failure and in the dismissal of Burnside from his ill-fated command. His successor, General Joseph Hooker, was no more successful at Chancellorsville, where in May 1863 Union forces were turned back again by Lee; in action concluding on May 4 and 5, Lee concentrated his troops against Hooker at Salem Church, 4 miles west of Fredericksburg, and forced the Union commander to retreat across the Rappahannock. The Confederates' success was costly, however, for Jackson had been mistakenly fired on by his own men on the night of May 2, and he died 8 days later. The Wilderness (May 5–7) and Spotsylvania Court House (May 9–19) action in 1864 was more indecisive, as Grant attempted to move Union forces between Lee and Richmond; though not successful, Grant's strategy substantially weakened his adversary and set the pattern for the war of attrition in the months ahead. Two visitor centers, each containing a museum, are in the park: in Fredericksburg on U.S. 1 at the foot of Marye's Heights, and on the Chancellorsville battlefield 10 miles west of Fredericksburg on State 3.

For further information write: Box 679, Fredericksburg, VA 22401

JAMESTOWN NATIONAL HISTORIC SITE, *Jamestown Island*

After stopping briefly at Cape Henry, the colonists who established the first permanent English settlement in America built Jamestown beginning on May 13, 1607. It was the capital of the colony of Virginia from 1607 to 1698; it also was the scene of the meeting of the Virginia House of Burgesses in 1619—the first representative assembly in the New World. All the Jamestown area excluding the National Historic Site (which is privately administered) is included in Colonial National Historical Park. The only part of the settlement remaining above ground is **Old Church Tower,** dating from about 1640. But the visitor can see foundations of houses and public buildings (including three State Houses), remains of streets, and a variety of artifacts, all recently uncovered through archaeological research. Other early Jamestown landmarks and personages are visible through representations, including paintings and statues. **James Fort**, **Powhatan's Lodge**, and replicas of the ships that brought the colonists are among the representations in Jamestown Festival Park.

Open daily during daylight hours. For further information write: Superintendent, Colonial National Historical Park, Yorktown, VA 23490

MOUNT VERNON NATIONAL HISTORIC LANDMARK, *7 miles south of Alexandria on George Washington Memorial Parkway*

As a home site, this was patented by the Washington family in 1674. Lawrence Washington, half-brother of George, built the estate in his period of residence, beginning in 1743. George took possession in 1754, enlarged the main house, built a group of outbuildings, and landscaped the grounds, which now contain his grave. He resided in Mount Vernon until his call to lead American Revolutionary forces, again following the war, and finally during the period between the end of his Presidency (1797) and his death (1799). This famous estate is a treasure house of Washington memorabilia and a source of much information about early American life and society.

Open: Mar-Oct, daily 9–5; Nov-Feb, daily 9–4

PETERSBURG VICINITY

FIVE FORKS BATTLEFIELD NATIONAL HISTORIC LANDMARK, *12 miles west on County 627 at Church Road*

In this decisive engagement, April 1, 1865, Lee's last supply line in his defense of Richmond and Petersburg was cut. He dispatched General George E. Pickett to keep Federal forces from the Southside Railroad, but General Philip Sheridan's Union troops severed this vital supply route and forced Lee to withdraw from Richmond.

PETERSBURG NATIONAL BATTLEFIELD, *southeast, south, and southwest*

The 10-month Petersburg campaign, beginning in June, 1864, and ending at Five Forks *(see)*, was an ultimately successful Union effort to take this city, the vital depot through which supplies for the Confederate defense of Richmond flowed. Grant's dogged siege gradually constricted Lee's forces and supplies by rail. Petersburg's fall on April 3, 1865, thereby dooming Richmond, made Lee's surrender at Appomattox *(see)* inevitable. Still visible are many original earthworks used in the campaign; nearby is **Poplar Grove National Cemetery**, where many of the dead lie.

Visitor Center open: June-Labor Day, 8–7; rest of year, 8–5

George Washington's home at Mount Vernon was rescued—and is still run—by the Mount Vernon Ladies' Association of the Union.

MOUNT VERNON LADIES' ASSOCIATION

RICHMOND AND VICINITY

MARSHALL HOUSE NATIONAL HISTORIC LANDMARK, *Ninth and Marshall streets*

John Marshall, one of the most influential holders of the office of Chief Justice of the U.S. Supreme Court (1801—35), was owner of this brick house for 45 years and spent much of his life in it. The structure was built in 1790; an additional bedroom was provided in 1810.

Open: Tues-Sat 10–4

RICHMOND NATIONAL BATTLEFIELD PARK

The fall of the Confederate capital, Richmond, on April 3, 1865, was preceded by 7 Union drives. McClellan's **Peninsular Campaign of 1862** came close to success. Eventually Grant's siege of Petersburg *(see)*, 1864–65, resulted in the surrender of that key supply base and of Richmond. A complete tour of the related battlefields (of 1862 and 1864–65) requires a 97-mile drive; an abundance of earthworks, fortifications, and trenches remain. The park's main visitor center is at 3215 East Broad Street; other such centers are at 2 of the major combat sites; **Cold Harbor**, where Lee's repulse of Grant, June 3, 1864, caused the latter to concentrate his primary attention on Petersburg thereafter, and **Fort Harrison**.

For further information write: 3215 E. Broad St., Richmond, VA 23223

STATE CAPITOL (CONFEDERATE CAPITOL) NATIONAL HISTORIC LANDMARK, *Capitol Square*

This famous building, designed by Thomas Jefferson and Louis Clerisseau after the ancient Corinthian temple in Nîmes, France, the Maison Carrée, has been the state capitol for almost 200 years, and it was also the Confederate capitol during the years (1861–65) when Richmond was the capital of the Confederacy. It was built between 1785 and 1792; wings were added in 1904–5. In the Old Hall, Aaron Burr's treason trial was conducted in 1807. In the rotunda is the figure of George Washington by Jean Antoine Houdon; on the grounds of Capitol Square is the equally famous Washington Monument executed by Thomas Crawford from designs by Robert Mills.

Open: Apr-Nov, daily 9–5; Dec-Mar, Mon-Sat 9–5, Sun 1–5

WILLIAMSBURG AND VICINITY

CARTER'S GROVE NATIONAL HISTORIC LANDMARK, *1/5 mile southeast of the intersection of U.S. 60 and State 667*

This imposing Georgian mansion, which has been described as "the most beautiful house in America," was built between 1750 and 1753 and was remodeled and enlarged in 1927–28. The original owner was Carter Burwell, grandson of the noted Virginia landholder and colonial official Robert "King" Carter.

Open: March-Nov, daily 9–5

WILLIAMSBURG HISTORIC DISTRICT NATIONAL HISTORIC LANDMARK, *bounded by Francis, Waller, Nicholson, North England, Lafayette, and Nassau streets*

Originally settled in 1632 as Middle Plantation, Williamsburg was renamed in 1699, when it succeeded Jamestown as capital of the colony of Virginia. Restoration of a very famous historic district (Colonial Williamsburg) in a historic city began in 1927 and has striven to re-create the environment of the period when Wil-

liamsburg was a flourishing capital city (until 1799). Of particular historical interest are 3 reconstructions of buildings destroyed by fire and now used for exhibition purposes: the **Colonial Capitol**, Duke of Gloucester Street, on the foundations of the original (1705) building; **Governor's Palace**, Palace Green, home of Virginia's royal governors in colonial days; and **Raleigh Tavern**, adjoining the capitol, a center of social activity and then a meeting place for patriots as the Revolutionary era neared. Five structures separately designated National Historic Landmarks are within this district (itself an NHL): the **Wren Building** (1702) on the campus of the College of William and Mary, built on original designs by Sir Christopher Wren and now restored; **Bruton Parish Church** (1712–15), on Duke of Gloucester Street; the **Peyton Randolph House** (1715–24), Nicholson Street, most of whose interiors are original; **James Semple House** (about 1780), Francis Street, thought to have been designed by Thomas Jefferson; and **Wythe House** (1752), Palace Green, home of George Wythe (noted jurist and civic official and a signer of the Declaration of Independence) and headquarters for George Washington before the siege of Yorktown and for Rochambeau afterward. All but the Semple House are accessible to the public.
Bruton Parish Church open: Mon-Sat 10–5; services Sun. Information available at Information Center, northeast of the Governor's Palace

YORKTOWN BATTLEFIELD, *Colonial National Historical Park at U.S. 17*
Here, on October 19,1781, American independence was virtually secured with the successful conclusion of the American-French siege of Lord Cornwallis's British forces. Earthworks, mounted cannon, and other relics of the action have been preserved, and **Moore House**, where the articles of capitulation were drafted, has been restored. A visitor center at the eastern end of **Colonial Parkway** is the starting point of a self-guided tour. **Yorktown National Cemetery** is part of this site.
For further information write: Box 210, Yorktown, VA 23690

WASHINGTON

CHINOOK VICINITY
LEWIS AND CLARK CAMPSITE STATE PARK, *2 miles south on U.S. 101*
Captains Meriwether Lewis and William Clark, on their epoch-making trek across North America, first recorded the breakers of the Pacific Ocean at this site, where they camped from November 15 to 24, 1805. After a 17-month journey, the expedition entered the present state of Washington on October 11, 1805, and canoed down the Snake and Columbia rivers, portaging dangerous rapids along the way. (Today the **Lewis and Clark Trail Highway** follows their approximate route from Clarkston, at the Idaho border, to Ilwaco, at the mouth of the Columbia.) On November 17, Clark and 11 men left the campsite and proceeded along the beach to **Cape Disappointment** and the Pacific, thus achieving their principal goal.

SEATTLE

KLONDIKE GOLD RUSH NATIONAL HISTORICAL PARK, *headquarters at Pioneer Square*

This area was the heart of Old Seattle, which was first settled across Elliott Bay at Alki Point in 1851 and relocated in 1852 to its present site. A fine natural harbor and a vast expanse of virgin forest combined to make a new community—named Seattle after a local Indian chieftain, Sealth—an excellent setting for its first industry, a sawmill opened in 1853. Seattle prospered and within a half century became the major city of the Northwest. Although in 1889 a fire burned down Seattle's docks and most of its business district, the town was soon rebuilt with late Victorian structures. In 1897, 68 prospectors from the Klondike landed in Seattle and the famous Gold Rush was on. More stampeders left for the Yukon from Seattle than from any other city. It was here that they bought supplies and headed for Skagway in Alaska. Pioneer Square has been restored to its appearance at the time of the Gold Rush.

For further information write: National Park Service, Pacific Northwest Region, 2001 Sixth Ave., Seattle, WA 98121

The brick enginehouse from which John Brown and his followers battled Robert E. Lee's U.S. Marines had become a tourist attraction by the 1880s.

LIBRARY OF CONGRESS

WEST VIRGINIA

CHARLES TOWN

JEFFERSON COUNTY COURTHOUSE, *George and Washington streets*

The abolitionist John Brown was tried here and convicted of treason following his raid on the government arsenal at Harpers Ferry *(see)* in October 1859. He was hanged in Charles Town on December 2, 1859.
Open daily 9–5

HARPERS FERRY NATIONAL HISTORICAL PARK, *in Harpers Ferry*

This historic town developed from a settlement begun in 1733. In 1796 a Federal arsenal was built, and it was the abolitionist John Brown's raid on the arsenal, October 16–17, 1859, that stirred an entire nation. Seeking to establish both a stronghold for a frontal attack on the institution of slavery and a refuge for blacks, Brown and 18 followers seized several strategic points before a troop of Marines, commanded by Colonel Robert E. Lee, quelled the insurrection. Brown was routed from the enginehouse where he had barricaded himself. Tried in Charles Town *(see)*, he was convicted of treason and hanged. The park includes a district within Harpers Ferry that contains a visitor center, together with separate areas in **Loudoun Heights**, **Bolivar Heights** (both in West Virginia), and **Maryland Heights** (Maryland). High points of a walking tour include the **Master Armorer's House** (1859), restored home of the chief gunsmith of the armory, now a museum of gunmaking; **Brown's Fort**, the fire-engine house used by Brown on the armory site; and **Harper House** (1775–82), also restored, the oldest surviving structure within Harpers Ferry.
For further information write: Box 65, Harpers Ferry, WV 25425

WISCONSIN

BARABOO

RINGLING BROTHERS CIRCUS WINTER QUARTERS NATIONAL HISTORIC LANDMARK

Baraboo served as the winter home of the Ringling Brothers Circus from 1884 until 1918. Several of the old circus buildings survive and have been converted into industrial and commercial structures. Exhibits at the **Circus World Museum** re-create the history of circuses and include the world's largest collection of circus wagons.
Open: mid-May–mid-Sept, daily 9:30–6; mid-July–mid-Aug 9:30–8:30

WYOMING

CASPER VICINITY

INDEPENDENCE ROCK NATIONAL HISTORIC LANDMARK, *50 miles southwest on State 220*

Situated on the **Oregon Trail** near the Sweetwater River, this 193-foot-tall rock, covering 27 acres, served as a natural landmark for westward-bound pioneers. A favorite campsite, the rock became known as "the great registry of the desert" because of the numerous inscriptions left on it by travelers.

FORT BRIDGER STATE HISTORIC SITE, *off I-80 on Blacks Fork of the Green River*

Erected as a trading post in 1843 by the famous mountain man Jim Bridger, this fort became the second most important outfitting point—next to Fort Laramie *(see)*—for travelers on the overland route between the Missouri River and the Pacific Coast. From 1853 to 1857 Mormons held Fort Bridger, which they used as a supply base for their converts en route to Salt Lake City. The Federal government declared the post an official military reservation in 1858 and began an extensive building campaign. Early in the 1860s the fort served as a pony express and overland telegraph and stage station. From 1867 to 1869 Fort Bridger was an important supply center during the building of the Union Pacific Railroad, and the gold rush to the northwest. A military museum is on the site.
Open: May 15-Oct 15, daily 9–6; Oct 16-May 14, Sat, Sun 9–6

FORT LARAMIE NATIONAL HISTORIC SITE, *3 miles southwest of Fort Laramie off U.S. 26*

Serving initially as a major fur-trading center and later as a military post on the old **Oregon Trail**, Fort Laramie played an important role in the overland migrations to the West and in bloody Indian campaigns. Established in 1834 at the confluence of the Laramie and North Platte rivers, the outpost was sold to the American Fur Company in 1836. During the 1840s emigrant trains began stopping at Fort Laramie for supplies, and in 1849 the U.S. government purchased the post to protect travelers from hostile Indians. The installation served as a pony express and overland mail station in 1860–61 and was the scene of treaties signed by the Sioux, Cheyenne, and other Great Plains tribes in 1851 and 1868. The fort's last major Indian campaign occurred in 1876, when it was used as a base of operations against Sitting Bull and other rebellious Sioux chiefs. Fort Laramie was abandoned in 1890. Today 12 of the 21 extant historic structures have been restored.
Open: Memorial Day-Labor Day, daily 7–7; rest of the year, daily 8–4:30

YELLOWSTONE NATIONAL PARK, *northwest Wyoming, southeast Idaho, southwest Montana; headquarters at Mammoth Hot Springs*

On March 1, 1872, Congress set aside Yellowstone as the world's first national park. The first white man to visit the Yellowstone country was John Colter, a veteran of the Lewis and Clark expedition, who in 1807 made a midwinter trek through this wonderland of spouting geysers, boiling hot springs, and sputtering mud volcanoes. Reports by Ferdinand V. Hayden, watercolors by the artist Thomas Moran, and photographs by William H. Jackson, produced during 1871–72 expeditions to Yellowstone, were instrumental in convincing Congress that it should create this national park.
For further information write: Superintendent, Yellowstone National Park, WY 82190

Old Faithful obliged visitors to Yellowstone about 1920 just as punctually as it does today.

BETTMAN ARCHIVE